Oct. 1989

To: Dan

From: Dad & Mom

The Unsafe Sky

The Unsafe Sky

William Norris

W · W · NORTON & COMPANY
New York · London

Copyright © 1981 by William Norris

All rights reserved.

Printed in the United States of America.

Library of Congress Cataloging in Publication Data

Norris, William.
    The unsafe sky.

    1. Aeronautics—Accidents.   2. Airplanes—
Air worthiness.   I. Title.
TL553.5.N66   363.1'24   81–22423
ISBN 0–393–01596–3   AACR2

W.W. Norton & Company, Inc. 500 Fifth Avenue, New York, N.Y. 10110
W.W. Norton & Company Ltd. 37 Great Russell Street, London WC1B 3NU
1 2 3 4 5 6 7 8 9 0

For Betty
Who used to love to fly

Contents

Introduction
to a risky business

Air travel is very safe: any airline will tell you so. You need to look at the back of your ticket to find out just how much confidence they really have that they will get you there in one piece. There you will discover that if your flight stops in the United States, or if your airline is party to a 'special contract', your relatives can sue it in the event of your death for a princely $75,000 (£31,500 at the current rate of exchange) and no more. Out of that your next of kin will have to pay their legal fees. If you travel elsewhere, or have been unwise enough to choose an airline which does not have a 'special contract', just pray that you reach your destination safely. If you don't, the value of your life can be as low as £4200. This is what is known as the Warsaw Convention.

What are you doing, entrusting your life to people who have so little confidence in their aeroplanes that they need to safeguard themselves in this way? If flying is really so safe, why do they need the Warsaw Convention?

Perhaps the question is better left unasked. You need to travel, you bought the ticket, and they have you. If we all stopped to read the small print, the queues at airline ticket desks would become intolerable. There is one piece of good news, though the small print does not mention it: since 1975 all British airlines have been required by law to have special contracts increasing their liability to not less than £24,000, exclusive of costs. It is a slightly macabre incentive to fly the flag, and due to be increased during 1981 to £55,000.

Now for the bad news. The Warsaw Convention has been frequently amended since it was signed in 1929, and at Guatemala in 1971 it was decided that something should be done to increase compensation for dead and injured passengers. Twenty-one nations, including Britain and the United States, signed a protocol which raised the permissible limit to more than £70,000. This was to increase automatically at five-year intervals, so that the compensation payable in 1981 would have been £87,750. Still not a great sum for a life, but quite an improvement.

Unfortunately, before this protocol could come into effect, it had to be ratified by the countries concerned. Ten years later, neither Britain nor the United States has done so. The new £50,000 limit may look generous, but it is only just over half what was agreed ten years ago.

Still, what is there to worry about? There can be no field of human activity in which so much time, effort and money is devoted to the cause of safety. All over the world there are committees, authorities, foundations, associations, inspectors, researchers, engineers and scientists devoting their lives to making flying safe. Millions are spent by governments and airlines.

The modern airliner is a marvel of technology, as safe as man can make it, and the men who fly it are highly trained, vastly experienced, constantly checked. They are guided through the skies by a sophisticated network of radar control which bears the same relation to the early days of air travel as a cruise on the QEII bears to the first voyage of Columbus.

And yet . . .

Airliners still fly into mountains, the ground and each other with monotonous regularity. They overshoot, undershoot and catch fire. That neo-God in the cockpit with four rings on his sleeve can make very human mistakes. People die. True, the crashes are fewer, in proportion to the number of flights, than they used to be. On the other hand, larger aircraft mean that a single crash can now result in the deaths of several hundred people.

There is no shortage of statistics to convince the nervous that flying is the safest form to travel. Try a few for size. In 1978, US airlines completed 99.99991 per cent of their flights without a fatality. In the whole of the Western world, in 1979, around 800 million passengers travelled by air, and only 1,267 of them (plus 149 crew members) were killed. This makes the odds against being killed in an air crash 565,000 to 1, which is probably better than you could get from a bookmaker on the chances of crossing a busy road in one piece. To put it another way, there are roughly two fatal accidents per million departures in the West (the Eastern Bloc keeps its accident rate a secret) and some major air transport countries – among them Britain and the US – do even better.

Not much to worry about there – unless you happened to be one of the 1,267, in which case it is too late. However, it is worth noting that the fatality figure for 1978 was only 962, but that in the first six months of 1980 there had already been 739 deaths. The odds seem to be getting shorter.

Each year in the United States, the National Transportation Safety Board (NTSB) produces statistics which show the number of fatal accidents for each mode of transport. Take 1979: in that year 51,083 people died on the roads of the United States, compared with 353 who met their death on scheduled airliners. 614 were killed on the railways and 878 at level crossings. There now, doesn't that prove the point? If figures mean anything at all, those have to show that it is safer to fly than to drive your car, or even travel by train.

It all depends how you look at the figures. Let us take another year, 1975, in which the number of airline fatalities in the US was exceptionally low at 124. Now examine the occupant fatality rate per 100 million vehicle miles. For scheduled airline passenger it works out at 4.9. Passenger cars had only 2.6 fatalities on this basis, and all road transport (including motor cycles) 3.4. Trains only killed 1.3 passengers per 100 million miles.

Both sets of figures are equally accurate. You may begin to see what Disraeli meant when he spoke of 'lies, damned lies, and statistics'. Another pretty comparison, much loved by airline public relations men, is the fact that as many people are killed on the roads in the United States every eight days as die in airline accidents throughout the world in a year. In Britain the same thing happens every fifty-two days.

In the West, at least, there is no hiding the accidents on which these statistics are based. An air crash is a horrifying disaster that makes instant headlines. But accidents are not the whole story. Dreadful as they are, they make up only a minute proportion of the things which go wrong on airlines. The balance, the unseen bulk of the iceberg beneath the sea of complacency which surrounds air safety, are known as *incidents*. An incident can be as minor as a faulty instrument or as major as a pressurization failure. It differs from an accident only in degree; through sound design, the skill of the pilot, or sometimes pure blind chance, nobody was hurt.

Incidents rarely become public knowledge. Facts about them are jealously guarded from the fare-paying passengers by airlines, manufacturers and even such public bodies as the Civil Aviation Authority. Their reticence is understandable because the total is formidable, and there is too much money at stake for the sort of total frankness that might drive away the customers. It is also true that the details of many incidents are too technical or too capable of misinterpretation to be of much use to the public. But this hardly excuses the lamentable failure of many within the industry to spread news of their troubles among themselves. There are honourable exceptions within the industry who do their best – among them British Airways – but there is no overall exchange of information. The reason is fear; fear of becoming legally liable at some future date if the declared incident should recur and cause an accident. When an accident actually happens, this fear of legal redress can become a blind panic, leading to cover-ups which can obstruct an investigation and possibly lead to further disasters. Failure to exchange information has caused many deaths, as we shall see.

There is no denying that a high percentage of incidents are, of themselves, too trivial to cause serious concern. Yet the history of aviation is littered with examples of minor problems which escalated into major disasters through lack of knowledge or attention. Benjamin Franklin's adage, 'A little neglect may breed mischief' was never more true than it is of aviation.

This book is an attempt to let a little light into the dark places, not only in the belief that those who buy their tickets have a right to know what is going on, but also in the hope that public awareness may concentrate the minds behind the closed doors. All the facts I use are from authoritive sources. Some have been provided freely, some unwillingly and some, I confess, unknowingly. Fortunately there are those in the aviation industry who put the interests of safety above commercial and political considerations or bureaucratic rules. For fear of reprisals they must remain anonymous, but I would like to thank them for their help.

It is a sad fact that 355 jet airliners have been lost since 1959, representing 6.45 per cent of the present fleet of 5000 aircraft. According to one forecast, given at the

Flight Safety Foundation seminar in October 1980, a further 115 will crash fatally by 1986. Of these, nineteen are expected to be lost in 1981, including five in Europe and five in the United States. At least two will be wide-body jets which can carry up to 480 passengers.

These figures are not yet statistics. It is earnestly to be hoped that they will prove to be lies. But unless the iceberg is exposed, unless everyone concerned with aviation safety is made aware of what is happening to everybody else, the chances are slim that these disasters will be averted. To quote Mr Webster Todd, former chairman of the NTSB: 'Aviation's greatest accident is that there are not more accidents.' It is a chilling thought.

1

Too close to heaven

For pilots and controllers alike, the mid-air collision is the ultimate nightmare. However vast and empty the sky may look to a layman gazing upwards, the risk is ever present. The convergence of traffic at major airports, the often unpredictable movement of light aircraft – especially in the United States and Western Europe – and any lapse of concentration in air-traffic control, are all major hazards. Once two aircraft have collided, there is very little hope of survival; only the long fall to earth which must take an eternity. For those who must view the result, the after-math of any crash is harrowing; but these are the worst. As one seasoned investigator told me, 'If the plane hits a mountain, at least you know that they knew nothing about it. But these poor devils (and he named a particular crash) knew what was going to happen all the way down.'

Tremendous effort goes into the avoidance of such disasters, and modern aids and techniques have at least kept pace with the growth of traffic to keep the danger in check. But the problem refuses to go away. For all the regulations that are aimed at keeping aircraft 5 miles apart horizontally and at least 1000 feet vertically, incidents still happen. What is more, they happen very frequently indeed. Actual collisons are thankfully rare, but 'air misses' – close encounters of very undesirable kind – are an almost commonplace event.

In the United Kingdom alone, where the tightly con-trolled airspace and the relatively small number of private aircraft make the problem less acute, there are an average of 200 airmisses reported every year. There may be more which go unreported, because by definition an airmiss report is filed only when a pilot considers he has been definitely endangered by the proximity of another aircraft. Some pilots interpret this more liberally than others: I know one who insists that it is not worth reporting unless he can actually recognize the man in the other cockpit. Not all these incidents involve an actual risk of collision but a significant number do, and considerable efforts are made to prevent news of them reaching the public. It is extremely unlikely that the average reader will have heard any of the stories which follow in this chapter.

One of the problems about learning the details of near collisions, and hence gaining knowledge which might help to prevent similar happenings, is that the vast majority happen through human error on the part of pilot or controller. Put it this way: if you had just driven through a red light and got away with it, would you seek out the next traffic policeman and tell him what you had done? That is what pilots and controllers, whose careers may be at stake, are expected to do. Like the rest of us, they are only human.

In Britain, or so it is believed by the authorities, the problem has been pretty well solved. An independent body known as the Joint Airmiss Working Group, jointly sponsored by the Civil Aviation Authority and the Ministry of Defence, sits to consider all the near collisions in British airspace. Only the chairman knows the names of the pilots involved or the companies for which they fly. All such information is deleted before the group even considers the case.

There are nine permanent members, under the chairmanship of an RAF Group Captain from the National Air Traffic Services, and they represent both military and civilian interests. On the civil side, there are representatives from British Airways, IATA, the British Airline Pilots Association, the Guild of Air Pilots, and the General Aviation Safety Committee. The four Service members come from Support and Strike Commands of the RAF, the Ministry of Defence flight safety organization, and the procurement executive for research and development flying.

Details of all incidents, together with the group's conclusions, are circulated every four months to a restricted list of people in the aviation world. Again, all means of identification are excluded and the following warning appears on the title page of each report: 'This Analysis is for Official Use Only. The contents are not to be released to the public and are not to be discussed with the press without the authority of the Joint Field Commander, Field Headquarter, National Air Traffic Services.' Such authority, I can say from personal experience, is not given.

The reason appears to be two-fold. In the first place, there must be genuine concern that publicity would make those involved reluctant to report, even if names were still excluded. Secondly, apart from endemic civil service secrecy, there is a reluctance to have the travelling public scared out of its wits.

Those of a nervous disposition should read no further.

One afternoon in the spring of 1979 a DC10 of Laker Airways with a seating capacity of 380 took off from Prestwick Airport in Scotland and headed west across the Atlantic. Its destination was Detroit, Michigan. For the passengers enjoying their drinks as the advance-booking charter flight climbed to its cruising height of 31,000 feet, there was nothing out of the ordinary. Ireland slipped away on the port side and the DC10 joined North Atlantic air route Bravo, heading towards its next landfall at Gander, Newfoundland.

A few days earlier a DC10 of American Airlines* had crashed at O'Hare Airport, Chicago, after an engine had fallen from the wing on take-off. It was the worst aviation accident the United States had ever known, with a death toll of 273, and the Federal Aviation Administration was under intense public pressure to do something, anything. What the FAA did, on 29 May, was to ground all DC10 aircraft under its jurisdiction and to ban all those owned by foreign airlines from landing in the United States.

It was an unprecedented action, born of panic, which cast grave doubts on the design and construction of the DC10. No matter that after the full investigation these proved to be unfounded; the damage was done. Laker Airways, which had bought a fleet of DC10s for its infant Skytrain service, was clearly going to be badly hit by the ban. But at the moment it was imposed the airline had a more immediate problem: a DC10 over the Atlantic with nowhere to go.

After urgent consultations by radio on the company channel, the pilot agreed to turn round and head back for England and the Laker base at Gatwick. It must have been a marginal decision because by this time the flight was more than halfway across the ocean, approaching the southern tip of Greenland. Clearance was obtained from the air-traffic controller at Gander to make a 180-degree turn and fly back down the same air route. The plan was to follow route Bravo to its eastern junction at 56N 10W and then turn southeast to Gatwick. The comments of the passengers on this unexpected turn of events have not been recorded. No doubt they were graphic.

The Laker pilot requested permission to climb to 35,000 feet where he would use less fuel, but this was denied because of conflicting traffic. He continued at

* See Chapter 13.

31,000 feet and headed steadily towards home. At the end of route Bravo, at 8.45 p.m., he made his routine report to the Scottish Air Traffic Control Centre and requested confirmation of his inbound course to Gatwick. With the setting sun behind its tail, the huge airliner gently dipped its starboard wing and settled on to a new course of 140 degrees to the southeast. Unknown to those on board, it was no longer alone in the sky.

A short while before, a Lockheed C5 Galaxy of the United States Air Force had taken off from Mildenhall in East Anglia bound for America. The Galaxy, largest transport aircraft in the world with a wingspan of 223 feet, had been guided by the London Air Traffic Control Centre towards Belfast on airway UK3. At 8.40 p.m. it was handed over to the Scottish sector 26 controller – the same controller who was due to take charge of the Laker DC10 nine minutes later. The Galaxy was instructed to hold its position over Belfast until it could be allocated a North Atlantic route. Two minutes later the new clearance came through: the Galaxy was authorized to join route Bravo at 56N 10W. Its altitude was 31,000 feet.

The scene had been set. There were now two vast aircraft travelling along the invisible road in the sky in opposite directions, with hundreds of souls on board. Their closing speed was 1100 miles per hour.

Over the western horizon the sun was beginning to set. The Laker pilot scanned the darkening sky to the east. Suddenly he gasped with alarm. Only 300 yards ahead, appearing from nowhere, the gigantic bulk of the Galaxy was heading straight towards him. There was no time for any avoiding action. Like two enormous bullets, the aircraft passed each other in a split second. The most spectacular mid-air collision in history had failed to happen by a mere 750 feet. This was an estimate agreed by the pilots as, badly shaken, they continued on. It could have been less. It is doubtful that the passengers even noticed.

How could such a thing have happened in the highly disciplined environment of British airspace? The weather was clear, both pilots were highly professional and both were obeying to the letter their instructions from the ground. An investigation by the Joint Airmiss Working Group came up with two conclusions. First, the sector 26 controller had, 'for some inexplicable reason', failed to notice the potential conflict between the two aircraft displayed on his flight progress strips*. And second, the Oceanic planning controller at LATCC should not have cleared the Galaxy to proceed at 31,000 feet without consulting the sector 26 controller.

In other words, air-traffic control got it wrong, and got away with it. The group's terse report leaves no doubt about how close it was. It records: 'At such high closing speeds there was little that could be done to avert a collision. In the event, it was purely fortuitous that adequate horizontal separation existed and the risk of collision was thought to have been very serious.'

By chance, there was no collision, and the relatives of those on the Laker flight were saved an awkward legal battle with the Warsaw Convention. Would the DC10 have been deemed to be en route to the US, in which case they would have qualified for the $75,000 per head, or would it count as a flight from Prestwick to Gatwick, bringing a much-reduced level of compensation? Could they have sued the CAA for vectoring the aircraft on a collision course? We shall never know. And it is worth remembering that if the authorities had had their way, we should never have know that the incident happened at all.

How many more have there been? The figures, as opposed to details of the incidents, are not too difficult to come by if you know where to look. They disclose that in

*See Chapter 3.

1979 twenty-nine airliners were involved in twenty-three incidents in British airspace in which there was a real risk of disaster. Forget about light aircraft, military aircraft and occasions when two planes merely came too close for comfort. These were twenty-nine flights on which you and I might have bought a one-way ticket to the grave. Still, this was better than in the preceding two years, in each of which forty-two airliners were involved in such incidents. Take comfort: in 1977, for every million hours flown in the UK, there were 106 serious airmisses. By 1979 the figure had come down to 61 per million.

The powers-that-be in the CAA are reasonably frank about the overall position, though their mouths slam shut like lift doors if you ask for any details of airmisses. Air Vice Marshal Ian Pedder is Deputy Controller of the National Air Traffic Service, known in the trade as NATS. 'There are airmisses going on,' he told me, 'and people are at risk when these happen. Over the last fifteen years the traffic has doubled and the number of airmisses has halved, but there is an irreducible minimum which will only be dropped off if people never get airborne. The majority of time we are dealing with human beings: either pilots, controllers, or people like me responsible for airspace design, who have made a balls of it. It is the nature of the beast that we probably cannot reduce it to zero. All we can do is to try to learn from every air miss as to how we should get it better in the future.'

So there you are: these things happen and they are going to go on happening. Just utter a small prayer that they will not happen to you – and be thankful that were not on board one of two Boeing 747 jumbo jets flying over southern England in the autumn of 1977.

The confidential report on this incident does not give the exact date nor the identity of the airlines involved, though reliable sources in the United States tell me that one was German and the other American. It hardly matters. The facts which the report does reveal are horrific enough to be going on with. One of the 747s was heading from New York to Frankfurt, the other from Frankfurt to New York, and both were under the control of the Bristol sector controller at the London Air Traffic Control Centre at West Drayton. The inbound flight was flying at 33,000 feet and was cleared to descend to 29,000 feet by the time he reached Woodley navigational beacon, which stands on a disused airfield just to the east of Reading.

It is standard procedure that air-traffic control instructions are repeated back by the pilot in order to avoid mistakes, but on this occasion the 747 pilot noticed that the controller did not seem to be receiving his reply. He switched to another frequency to confirm the instruction, and the descent began. It was 7.42 a.m.

At 07.43 the second 747, heading northwest from Frankfurt, made radio contact with the controller. At this point it was 110 miles away from the incoming jet and not yet on the Bristol controller's radar screen. It was just then that things started to go wrong.

Like the cause of so many potential air disasters, the initial fault was simple and unpredictable. It happened many miles away at Clee Hill in Shropshire, which is a long-range airspace surveillance station. The Clee Hill transmitter, operating on 133.6 MHz, became jammed in the transmit position. Since the same frequency was being used to control the 747s, communication between them and the Bristol controller was effectively blocked. True, the pilot of the incoming aircraft had managed to re-establish contact on another frequency, but this meant that he was speaking to a different controller who was not responsible for that sector. The latter had to send a messenger across the room to confirm the descent clearance before he could pass it back to the pilot.

The Bristol sector controller, of course, had no means of knowing why his transmissions were not getting through. He tried and tried on 133.6 MHz while the Clee Hill transmitter momentarily cleared and then jammed again, and the minutes ticked by. The 110 miles which had separated the two aircraft were being rapidly eroded as they sped towards each other at a closing speed of 1000 m.p.h. At 07.48 they were only sixteen miles apart.

It was now that an element of tragic farce began to enter the affair. The Bristol sector controller was a short man and in order to reach his stand-by r/t handset, suspecting the main equipment was at fault, he had to stand up and reach over his horizontal radar screen. He was thus unable to see the two blips creeping closer and closer on a collision course. It was the second controller who noticed something was wrong. The two jumbos were only seven miles apart when he saw the danger, and he at once passed new instructions to the pilot of the incoming aircraft.

In what was later described as 'a calm, normal, matter-of-fact manner' he instructed the pilot to hold his descent at 31,500 feet and to turn left 30 degrees. There was no reason given, no suggestion of urgency. Nevertheless the pilot did his best to comply. Jumbo jets have many virtues, but mid-air agility is not one of them. By the time the pilot had managed to stop his descent and make the turn he had reached 31,200 feet. It was almost too late. As the great nose swung to port, he confronted the other 747 head-on. It was so close that it filled his entire front windshield panel. He did the only thing he could, steepening the turn to the left and taking instant evasive action. The other Boeing, which seconds before had been alerted by the now-aware Bristol sector controller to turn left immediately, did likewise. The two giants missed each other by about 300 feet, and a major disaster just failed to go into the record books.

The jumbo passengers were lucky: on this occasion the pilots had just sufficient warning to use their skill and turn tragedy into a non-event. Often it is otherwise. The speeds are so great and the distances so small that there is no time for a pilot to react. Sometimes one or other pilot is even unaware until later that anything was amiss.

Take the case of the Boeing 707 and the Douglas DC8, both owned by non-British airlines, which so nearly came to earth near the peaceful Sussex town of Midhurst in the summer of 1977. It had been a quietish night in the London Air Traffic Control Centre and the morning shift had just come on duty. There was not much traffic about at 6 a.m., but the controller for the Seaford/Worthing/Hurn sector had recently taken charge of two high-flying passenger jets crossing the country in their allotted air-lanes.

One was a DC8 flying eastwards on Upper Red One – an airway which crosses the Channel coast near Bournemouth and swings right across Hampshire and Sussex into the London Terminal control area. The DC8 was flying at 37,000 feet, the same height as a Boeing 707 which was making its way to the southeast down airway Upper Amber One.

These two airways intersect over Midhurst and, on the 'flight progress strips' which controllers use to keep track of where aircraft are going, both flights were due at the junction at the same time: 06.19.

There are no 'give way' signs at airway junctions and aircraft which stop to let the other fellow through tend to fall out of the sky. That is why air-traffic controllers exist. On this occasion, one aircraft or the other should have been told to slow down or been given a different height. In fact, nothing was done. The night-shift controller forgot to tell his relief that the two flights were in conflict; the new man simply failed to noticed what was happening on the radar screen. The two four-engined jets were left to speed towards the intersection in total ignorance.

Suddenly, as if from nowhere, the 707 pilot saw the DC8 flash across his nose from right to left and disappear. It had missed him by a scant 200 yards. As for the DC8, its pilot never even saw the Boeing. The first the ground controller knew of it was when the 707 pilot, having got his breath back, aroused him with an angry message at 06.21.

The subsequent Airmiss Working Group report said: 'All the information necessary to prevent this incident was available to the controller, both on the radar tube and on the flight progress strips, but for some unknown reason, account was not taken of it.'

The controllers in this instance were both experienced men – which would have been scant consolation if the laws of chance had not taken over at the last moment – but your flight will not always be managed by such people. Like those in any other skilled profession, controllers have to be trained, and part of their training has to be 'on the job'. Not that this is done without supervision. Two trainee controllers in charge of the Lydd and Dover sectors at LATCC were both being supervised one afternoon in the autumn of 1976 when they almost succeeded in ramming a BAC111 with a DC9.

The 111 was heading inbound to Luton from the Continent at 14,000 feet; the DC9 was climbing out of Heathrow on course for Dover. Both had to pass over a navigation beacon at Detling, which was where they met. The Dover trainee's instructor, who had been distracted by something else, suddenly realized that his charge was climbing the DC9 into the path of the 111. He instructed him to make the pilot turn, and so he did – the wrong way. The other instructor, seeing what was happening, decided that any action on his part would only make matters worse. The four controllers watched in horror as the two blips merged on the radar screen . . . and then with relief as they separated.

The 111 pilot only saw the DC9 at the last moment, 200 yards away on his port side and turning towards him. There was no time for any avoiding action, and the aircraft missed each other by perhaps 100 yards.

The inability to tell left from right is, of course, a common human failing – though not one to be easily excused in air-traffic controllers. In the spring of 1978 a trainee controller on his very first day made a similar error and almost collided two Tridents near Southampton

However, not all airmisses are the fault of controllers. Mistakes can also occur in the cockpit and, while this happens more frequently among less experienced pilots of light aircraft who lose their way and blunder into controlled airspace, the risk to airline passengers is just as great. Take the case of the unknown idiot who almost flew his Piper Cherokee into the side of a BAC111 as it was landing at Gatwick on 27 July 1979.

The 111 had just completed a flight from Newcastle and was making its final approach down the instrument-landing beam. It was 5 miles from touchdown at a height of 1500 feet when suddenly radar told the pilot of a contact on his right-hand side. He turned his head and saw it at once: a white single-engined Cherokee with a narrow red stripe along its side. It was heading straight for him, only 500 feet away. Both aircraft turned at the same moment – fortunately in the right direction – and the collision was avoided. The 111 landed safely and the Cherokee disappeared into the early morning mist. Its pilot has never been traced so his views are unknown, but the captain of the 111 put the risk of collision at 99 per cent.

The difficulty of tracing errant small aircraft is a recurring problem for the Joint Airmiss Working Group. Another is the widely differing accounts which pilots give of the same incident. In January 1979, for example, a near collision was reported between a Boeing 727 on its way from Gatwick to Alicante and a Boeing 747 outbound from Heathrow to Paris. Through a good deal of confusion in air-traffic control, which included a controller using the wrong call sign for the jumbo and hence getting no response, the radar blips of the two aircraft came together 12 miles southeast of Dunsfold.

The merging of radar returns, even if it does not necessarily denote a collision, is certainly too close for comfort when the two aircraft are known to be at about the same height. The captain of the 747, however, was completely unperturbed. He saw the 727, he said, when it was three miles away. It passed no closer than a mile, and with a height separation of about 1000 feet. There had been no risk of collision.

The 727 pilot's version was somewhat different. He claimed that the 747 passed directly underneath him at a distance of no more than 500 feet and with a very high risk of impact. Who was telling the truth?

We shall never know; just as we shall never be quite sure what happened in the summer of 1977 when a Boeing 707 and a twin-engined Boeing 737 almost met in cloud over Essex. The 707 pilot reported that as he was climbing through 8000 feet the other aircraft suddenly appeared in his windshield, crossing right to left in a descending turn. It was, he said, no more than 50 to 100 yards away at exactly the same height. The pilot of the 737, however, never even saw the other aircraft. He said later that while flying in cloud he was given two rather large and abrupt changes of heading by the controller and then asked if he would like to file an airmiss report. He declined to do so.

Given the speed of modern aircraft and the volume of traffic, it is perhaps not surprising that they sometimes come too close to each other. But surely they should be safe from collision on the runway? Not so. The worst air disaster on record happened at Tenerife on 27 March 1977 when one Boeing 747 ran into another during its take-off run, killing 575 passengers and crew. The facts of that accident are too well known to need repetition here, but how many people have heard of the disaster which nearly overtook a British Airways Viscount as it took off on a routine flight from Leeds to London on the morning of 6 November 1978? There was fog about (as there had been at Tenerife) when the pilot of flight BA5403 taxied his four-engined turbo-prop from the terminal to the runway. As he reached the take-off point, visibility had improved from 200 to 850 yards and he got take-off clearance from the tower. Prudently, because of the poor visibility, the pilot held the aircraft on its brakes until full power had been achieved. It was just as well. As the Viscount sped along the runway he saw a 'box-like shape' ahead of him. He took it to be a radio hut at the end of the runway, but he was wrong. As the Viscount reached 85 knots – too slow to fly, too fast to stop – the pilot realized that what he had seen was a fire engine facing towards him in the middle of the runway.

The captain did the only thing he could: he decided to take off. Hauling back on the control column, he dragged the reluctant Viscount into the air. Two firemen jumped for their lives as the fuselage just cleared their heads, and a planeload of lucky commuters staggered into the air and safety.

The cause of this particular incident was later put down to poor r/t procedure between the fire engine, which had been passing reports on runway visibility, and the control tower. However, the lesson has been learned. At Leeds Airport, at least, fire engines no longer patrol the runway on foggy days.

★

In spite of the incidents which can and do occur in British airspace, passengers can take comfort from the fact that things are better ordered there than on the Continent. Unless, that is, they happen to be flying in that direction.

West Germany is the most dangerous area, due to the large numbers of light aircraft, gliders and military planes all using the same airspace as airliners. British Airways alone had 17 near misses over Germany in 1978, 14 in 1977 and no fewer than 27 in 1976. In Europe as a whole the airline reported 294 air misses during this three-year period, plus 168 air-traffic control incidents in which controllers allowed aircraft to come closer to each other than they should. And those are the reports from only one airline, albeit a big one. How many near disasters are there over Europe in the course of any one year? Lacking any central reporting system, one can only guess, though British aircraft were involved in 99 such incidents in foreign airspace during 1980. The rest of Europe has no equivalent to the British Joint Airmiss Working Group. Under the rules of the International Civil Aviation Organization (ICAO) each country is supposed to have an airmiss reporting system, but most are state-controlled, far from comprehensive and even more shrouded in secrecy than the British set-up.

This is not the only ICAO rule which appears to be honoured more in the breach than the observance. Another, which bears directly on the problem of the mid-air collision, is the convention which lays down that English shall be the only language spoken between pilots and air-traffic controllers. Whatever the French may think, and they are one of the prime offenders against the rule, this is not a xenophobic Anglo-Saxon plot, but plain common sense. Virtually all airline pilots do speak English – even the Russians no longer use flight-deck interpreters on their flights to the West – and they need to understand not only the communications directed at them but also those affecting aircraft in their vicinity.

However, in recent years many European controllers have taken to talking to their own national aircraft in their own national language. The French began it, naturally, and the habit was taken up by Spaniards, Greeks and Yugoslavs. The British pilots who fly over Europe, and especially those landing at the Mediterranean holiday resorts, take extra care. They know that not only will they be going to airports which, in most cases, have no approach radar facilities, but also that the gibberish in their earphones may be directed at another aircraft on a collision course with their own. They have no way of knowing.

In the opinion of many pilots I have spoken to, this flouting of the ICAO rule is tantamount to criminal folly. It would be good to get the view of the British Airways Trident captain on the London – Istanbul flight of 10 September 1976, but he is dead. So are his fifty-four passengers and eight crew, and the 108 passengers and five crew of the Inex Adria DC9 which took off from Split that morning.

The accident was simplicity itself. The Trident, over-flying Yugoslavia at 33,000 feet on its way to Turkey, contacted Zagreb Air Traffic Control Centre at 10.14. The pilot estimated that he would be over Zagreb ten minutes later. Meanwhile the DC9 had taken off at 9.48, cleared to climb to 35,000 feet on a course which also took it over the Zagreb navigation beacon.

When he spoke to the pilot of the Trident, the Yugoslav controller forgot about the clearance issued to the DC9. He should have ordered some change of course or altitude to maintain separation, but he did not. It was only when the DC9 was passing through 32,500 feet that he realized his mistake. He told the Yugoslav pilot of the other plane in front of him, and he told him to stop climbing. But he told him in Serbo-Croat. The Trident captain, who might well have been able to take avoiding action had he known what was going on, was blissfully unaware that anything was wrong. Seconds later, everyone on board was dead.

The problem in Yugoslavia still exists; in the summer of 1980 British pilots were warned to take especial care after two near misses involving British Airways jets. On 14 June, a VC10 flying from Cairo to London at 31,000 feet passed within 150 yards of an Air France Boeing 707 going the other way. In the second incident, on 24 June, a Trident 2 was flying over Zagreb when the pilot noticed a Yugoslav DC10 close beside him at the same height. He reported the fact to the Zagreb controller, who promptly instructed him to turn right – an action which would have put him on a direct collision course with the DC10.

The Trident pilot, not to mention his unknowing passengers, was lucky; he could see the other aircraft. But what if the same incident had happened in cloud? As an example of what can happen when air-traffic controllers get it wrong, consider the events at Los Rodeos airport, Tenerife, on 25 April 1980.

Los Rodeos was not a favourite airport for pilots even before the tragedy of March 1977. Set high among mountains, it has no approach radar and is subject to sudden fogs when the cloud clamps down. After the collision between the two 747s a new airport, the Queen Sophia, had been opened at the southern end of the island, but in early 1980 Los Rodeos was still being used by British tour operators because it involved a shorter road transit to the island's holiday resorts.

Three aircraft had left England for Tenerife on the morning of 25 April. Two of them, a Dan-Air Boeing 727 from Manchester with 146 passengers and crew, and a

British Airtours Boeing 707 from Gatwick carrying 133 passengers and eight crew, were bound for Los Rodeos. The third, a Boeing 737 of Britannia Airways, was heading from Gatwick to Queen Sophia with close to its capacity of 130 passengers on board.

The Dan-Air 727, flown by Captain Arthur Whelan, was first in the queue as the three aircraft sped towards their destination. Behind him came the Britannia flight piloted by Captain John Oakes, with the Airtours 707 in the charge of Captain Pat Eadie bringing up the rear. Also on the flight deck with Captain Eadie and his co-pilot were two British air-traffic controllers who had been given a free flight to obtain experience. They were to get more than they bargained for. One of them, Miss Maria Quinn, was a senior controller from West Drayton, the other a junior officer from Gatwick.

The order changed *en route*. Some 150 miles out from the Canaries, Captain Eadie realized that he would be delayed on landing by the slower Britannia Airways aircraft. He asked for permission to overtake, and this was granted by Canaries air-traffic control. The 707 accelerated. When it reached the approach beacon at the northern end of the island it was only about five minutes behind Captain Whelan's 727, and flying at 11,000 feet.

It was at this point that confusion began to creep in. The two aircraft had been told by Canaries control that the wind on Los Rodeos was blowing at 12 knots from 300 degrees. They therefore expected to be landing on runway 30, the most usual runway, which has instrument-landing facilities. Cloud coverage was said to be 2/8 at 900 feet above the runway, and 3/8 at 1400 feet. There should have been no problems; but there were.

At the last minute, Los Rodeos approach control reported a change in the wind. It had turned right round and was now blowing from 160 degrees at 4 knots. In consequence, both flights were instructed to use runway 12, which is the same strip of tarmac but used in the opposite direction. Runway 12 at Los Rodeos, unlike runway 30, has no instrument-landing aids and no recognised 'holding pattern' for flights that cannot land at once. Nor is there any surveillance radar at the airport.

Present evidence suggests that Captain Whelan was about to cross the weak Fox Papa non-directional beacon at the end of runway 12, preparatory to turning right for the start of his landing approach, when a new factor entered the scene. The controller realized that there was insufficient separation behind an Iberian Airways Fokker Friendship about to land on 12, and issued new instructions to the Dan-Air flight. He ordered the 727 to enter a holding pattern, adding: "the standard holding overhead FP is inbound heading 150, turn to the left, call you back shortly."

The clearance seemed odd–a left turn would take the aircraft away from the approach end of the runway–but there was no pattern on Captain Whelan's chart to give guidance. He could not question the controller, because the latter was talking in Spanish to the pilot of the Friendship, and two aircraft cannot use the same radio channel at the same time. Poor Captain Whelan, whatever his position at that moment, must have been left in a state of uncertainty. But he did what he thought he was being told to do. He turned left.

This took him to the south of the airport, where the cloud was solid from 9,000 feet to about 2,000. At this point he was flying at 6,000 feet, blindly looking for a gap in the clouds that didn't exist. He was puzzled by the strange clearance, and worried by the stream of Spanish in his earphones which told him that there was another aircraft somewhere in the circuit. Then the controller cleared him to descend to 5,000 feet.

What happened next is unclear. At the time of writing the report of the official inquiry has yet to be produced. But there seems a high probability that Captain Whelan decided that he was much further from the runway threshold than he in fact was, and that mindful of high ground to his left he turned right again to make another circuit over the sea. If that was the case, it was a fatal mistake. Two minutes later the 727 struck the side of a mountain at 5,500 feet. Captain Whelan and all those on board died instantly.

No one saw the crash and no one at the airport had any inkling of what had happened. Having lost contact with the 727, the Los Rodeos controller asked the British Airtours captain to call up the missing aircraft on his own radio. Captain Eadie tried without success. In the meantime he obeyed an instruction to maintain his own altitude of 11,000 feet over the Fox Papa beacon, and looked at the cloud below. With no instrument-landing system, and a lost aircraft somewhere in the grey mass, runway 12 had become a very uninviting prospect. Captain Eadie requested permission to approach from the other end of the runway, from which he could make an instrument landing. He was cleared to fly parallel to the runway at 11,000 feet before joining the holding pattern for runway 30.

At this moment the Britannia Airways 737 entered the deadly game. Captain Oakes was descending towards Tenerife from the north, having been cleared by Canaries control, on a different frequency, to 11,000 feet. The two aircraft were now flying at right angles to each other on an exact collision course. For reasons unknown, the Los Rodeos controller said nothing.

If the cloud tops had been a little higher, nothing could have prevented a second crash over Tenerife that day.

Luckily they were not. Captain Oakes saw the danger as he was dropping through 12,000 feet, checked his descent and passed directly over the top of the 707.

As for Captain Eadie, he never saw the 737. Neither did his crew or the two air-traffic controllers on the flight deck as they dipped into the clouds to take up a holding pattern at 6000 feet. Their own troubles were not yet ended. After further unavailing attempts to contact the Dan-Air plane, the controller decided to close down the Los Rodeos runway and directed Captain Eadie to turn left on to the 213 degree radio beam from the nearby navigation beacon and to proceed to Queen Sophia airport. In fairness, had he had the advantage of radar and been able to see exactly where the 707 was at that moment, the controller would probably never have passed such an instruction. In fact it had just started another right-hand turn near the end of the runway. To have reversed that turn to the left, taking up a wide circle of sky, would have sent Captain Eadie and his passengers crashing into the side of a mountain long before they could rejoin the radio beam. It would have been the same mountain which had already claimed Captain Whelan.

The Airtours pilot had been to Tenerife many times before. He knew exactly where he was and where the instructed manoeuvre would take him. Wisely, he decided to turn right, ignoring the controller, and landed safely at Queen Sophia a few minutes later. Los Rodeos that day had seen its second major tragedy. But for the skill and concentration of two British pilots, it could have been much worse.

Not that pilots cannot make mistakes. They can and do, though the fact that their lives are just as much at stake as those of their passengers does tend to concentrate the mind wonderfully. Which is just as well. There is an ancient truism in aviation: there are old pilots and bold pilots, but very few old, bold pilots. Where near misses are concerned, their avoidance is very much a team matter between pilot and controller, and every now and again they both get it wrong – as happened near Ockham, Surrey, on the afternoon of 2 May, 1980.

The Fokker F28 Fellowship, a small twin-jet airliner which carries about eighty passengers, had taken off from Nantes that day *en route* for Heathrow. Under the instructions of Heathrow approach control it was executing a gentle right-hand orbit at 8000 feet around Ockham, when the pilot heard heard the sound of engines. They were not his own. Looking out he saw a Boeing 737 with red markings on the fuselage climbing through the bit of sky which he himself had occupied seconds before. A collision, he said later, had been missed by a miracle.

Such things are not supposed to happen on Britain's highly disciplined airways. What went wrong? Subsequent inquiry showed that it all began when the 737 took off from Heathrow and was cleared to 'climb to 5000 feet and 6000 feet to Seaford'. If this instruction had been followed, there would have been a separation of at least 2000 feet between the two aircraft, but on this occasion the captain decided to let his co-pilot fly the 737 to gain experience.

The co-pilot, to put it mildly, was not very good. He went up to 5000, down to 4000 and, on being instructed by the captain to conform to the procedures they had been cleared for, proceeded to climb straight through to 7000 feet.

On the ground, things were going wrong at the same time. After taking off, the pilot should have contacted London control's southwest departure controller on 132.05 MHz; in fact he called up on 125.8MHz which is the frequency used by the northeast sector controller. Realizing that a mistake had been made, the northeast controller tried to put it right – and then made a mistake of his own. He told the pilot to call up on 135.05MHz, which was the frequency of the Seaford controller.

It was 16.43. The Seaford controller had been expecting to hear from the 737, but not so soon. He could not see the aircraft on his radar screen, did not know at what height it was flying or what instructions had been given, and suspected something was wrong. Cautiously, he told the pilot to 'continue climbing as cleared, further climb very shortly.'

One minute later, for no apparent reason, the 737 pilot reported that he was passing 8000 feet. Had he suddenly seen the F28 and given himself a nasty fright? If he had, he never admitted it. Just after the incident took place he was asked by an anxious controller to what height he had been cleared by air-traffic control. There was no sensible reply. It was decided to let him carry on climbing up to 13,000 feet, out of harm's way.

In fact, under standard procedure, the 737 should only have been at 3000 feet when passing Ockham. It was the failure to stick to this rule, said the Joint Airmiss Working Group report, that had led to an incident 'which appeared to be extremely dangerous'. The group hoped 'that the B737's company would take steps to prevent a recurrence of such an incident'.

Neither the company nor the pilot were named in the report. They never are. By inference, the 737 was owned by a foreign airline (hence the failure of the co-pilot to understand what he ought to do), but that is as much as anyone will be permitted to know. The general public, of course, were to have been allowed to know nothing at all about an event which almost strewed wreckage and bodies over a large part of southern England.

This policy is defended by Air Vice Marshal Pedder:

Airmiss reports are valuable to us, and we need to get as many as we can. It is our judgement that if we then put the names and registration numbers on the reports and identify them, that people would not then report for one reason or another: either for insurances purposes, or because the pilot happened to be smoking his fag at the time. We have found both in civil and military reporting that a reasonable degree of anonymity is needed in order to get the maximum cooperation.

The British system, which has been working now for nearly twenty years, is operated on the joint thesis that voluntary cooperation is better than legal enforcement and that the more air misses are reported the more can be learned to prevent others. The possibility of litigation, which might well follow public exposure of the nastier events, is seen by Air Vice Marshal Pedder and his colleagues as leading inevitably to cover-up operations. And cover-ups are seen to be counter-productive to safety.

It is estimated (no one can be sure) that two-thirds of the dangerous near collisions in British airspace are in fact reported to the group. That may not seem a high proportion, bearing in mind the potential catastrophes which might lie in the remaining one-third, but it is still the envy of the rest of the aviation world. The price to be paid for this triumph of pragmatism over regulation is a high degree of public ignorance. But since secrecy is regarded as a positive virtue by the bulk of the civil service, inquiries on the subject are met by no more than a raised Whitehall eyebrow.

2
The cost of freedom

They order things differently across the Atlantic. The Federal Aviation Act of 1958 declares: 'There is hereby recognized and declared to exist on behalf of any citizen of the United States a public right of freedom of transit through the navigable airspace of the United States.' Thus, just as he jealously preserves the right to bear arms, the citizen can insist on freedom of the skies. Both rights can be equally lethal, but woe betide any American government which tries to abrogate them. Up to a height of 10,000 feet, the US private pilot can go where he likes and use the same airports as the big jets. Thousands of them do: 198,800 at the last count, and general aviation (as private flying is known) is responsible for 75 per cent of all air journeys in North America.

For airline pilots, and for air-traffic controllers, this is a constant headache. America is big, but not that big, and though the jets ride high to their destinations, they all have to start at ground level and come down again. Close to the airports, where the Cherokees and Apaches, the Navajos and Aztecs buzz and swarm, they have to pass through that crowded 10,000 feet of vertical airspace. The airline captains have a name for it. They call it 'Indian territory'.

There are no meaningful figures for the number of near misses which take place in the United States each year. The total certainly runs into thousands but the majority are never reported. The reason for this is the attitude of the Federal Aviation Adminstration, which relies on a set of rigid regulations rather than the policy of friendly persuasion practised by its British counterpart. If a pilot reports an air miss, even if he is not at fault, he has automatically infringed the FAA regulation which says that aircraft must maintain a certain separation. For this he could be fined or even suffer the suspension of his licence. In the past, few have felt inclined to take the risk.

The situation has changed somewhat since 1976 when NASA set up an air safety reporting system (ASRS) at the Ames Research Center near San Francisco. The purpose of the scheme was to get the maximum information on air misses and other safety incidents by offering pilots, controllers, and everyone else in the aviation industry, immunity from prosecution under FAA regulations if they would come forward with voluntary reports. The only exceptions, introduced under a later amendment to the scheme to prevent its abuse, are for those who violate the rules deliberately or who commit a criminal offence.

A measure of its success is that the ASRS attracted more than 17,000 reports in its first three years of operation – which is also an indication of the colossal problem which exists. The FAA, however, has been less than happy, for two reasons: first, its lawyers have been cheated of their prey; and second, the analyses of the reports produced by NASA have frequently shown that FAA personnel and procedures have been at fault when dangerous situations have developed. Hence the strenuous efforts made by the FAA to have the ASRS system wound up, almost since its inception. Happily for the sake of air safety these efforts have been unsuccessful, thanks to the opposition of practically the entire aviation community and a congressional committee on the subject. Those more concerned with saving lives than exacting a pound of flesh from those who make mistakes realize that only a free flow of information can prevent disasters like that which occured at San Diego 25 September 1978.

There is still quite a long way to go. Some experts estimate that N A S A is collecting no more than 20 per cent of the incidents which ought to be reported, though this can be no more than an educated guess. A further problem is that the A S R S reports, though considerably more accessible than those of their British equivalents (thanks to the Freedom of Information Act), are de-identified to such an extent that they sometimes become almost meaningless. When an incident becomes an accident and leads to injury or death, the whole situation changes. The investigators of the National Transportation Safety Board take over, and information flows freely.

The crash at San Diego, between a Boeing 727 of Pacific South West Airlines and a Cessna 172 light aircraft on an instrument-training flight, was a classic example of what can happen when general aviation traffic is allowed to share the airspace with the big boys.

Flight 182 had left Los Angeles for the short flight to San Diego at 08.34 that morning with 129 passengers and a crew of seven on board. The cockpit was crowded, with Captain James E. McFeron, his first officer Robert Fox, flight engineer Martin Wahne and another company pilot hitching a ride in the jump seat. Fox was actually flying the aircraft, while Captain McFeron handled the radio communications. He was an experienced pilot with more than 10,000 flying hours, 5800 of them on the 727.

The trip to San Diego is little more than a long-jump. Twenty minutes after take-off, flight 182 reported to approach control at 11,000 feet and was cleared to descend. Four minutes later, at 9500 feet, the captain reported the airfield in sight, and was authorized to make a visual approach to runway 27. There could have been nothing simpler: a fine day and no problems. Disaster was the last thing on anybody's mind.

The Boeing continued to descend towards Lindbergh Field, San Diego. Now it was in 'Indian territory'; the captain's earphones began to crackle with reports from the controller on other aircraft in the vicinity.

The approach controller at Lindbergh Field that day was Nelson E. Farwell. At 08.59.28 he warned Captain McFeron that there was traffic one mile in front of him headed north. 'We are looking,' the pilot replied, but he and his crew could see nothing. Eleven seconds later, Farwell told him of another aircraft nearby. This one was three miles distant just north of the field, climbing through 1400 feet to the northeast.

Fox and McFeron peered ahead and the co-pilot was the first to spot the light plane below them. 'Got 'em,' he said. 'Traffic in sight,' McFeron radioed to approach control, and was promptly cleared by Farwell to maintain visual separation and contact the Lindbergh tower for landing instructions. The brief flight had entered its routine final phase.

The second light aircraft on Farwell's radar screen (the first has never been identified) was a single-engined Cessna 172 – a common four-seater often used for training. It has a high wing, which gives excellent downward visibility but restricts the pilot's view above and to the side. This particular Cessna was owned by the Gibbs Flite Center, a local training school, and was being used that day to give instrument training to David Boswell. Boswell, with 407 hours under his belt, already held a commercial pilot's licence for single- and multi-engined aircraft. His instructor in the right-hand seat was Martin Kazy Jr. Kazy, who had worked for the Gibbs Flite Center for the past year, had flown 5137 hours, 347 of them in the past ninety days.

Pupil and instructor had taken off from nearby

Montgomery Field at 08.16, intending to practise instrument-landing approaches at Lindbergh. Everything had gone according to plan. When the Boeing began its descent, Boswell and Kazy had completed two landings and were climbing out again to the northeast. They were in contact with Lindbergh approach control, who told them stay below 3500 feet on a heading 070 degrees. At 09.00.31 Farwell, having handed over the Boeing to the tower, contacted Boswell and Kazy to warn them of its presence. He told them: 'Traffic at six o'clock, two miles, eastbound, a PSA jet inbound to Lindberg. Out of 3200. Has you in sight.' The Cessna acknowledged.

All was as it should be; everyone knew the location of everyone else in that clear blue sky. Or so it seemed.

Three seconds after the controller had spoken to the Cessna, Captain McFeron reported that the Boeing was on its downwind leg. The flaps went down and he asked his co-pilot, 'Is that the one we are looking at?'

'Yeah, but I don't see him now,' replied Fox. It was the first sign that anything might be going wrong, but there was no great concern in the cockpit of flight 182.

At 09.00.50 Captain McFeron transmitted to the controller, 'I think he's passed off to our right.' Two seconds later he said to Fox, 'He was right over there a minute ago.'

There was light conversation and laughter on the flight deck of the 727. The crew had not forgotten the presence of the Cessna but it did not seem to be dominating their minds. At 09.01.01, Fox, who was still flying the aircraft, asked 'Are we clear of that Cessna?'

'Supposed to be,' said the flight engineer.

'I guess,' said Captain McFeron.

From the occupant of the jump seat came a prophetic, 'I hope.'

But twenty seconds later, Captain McFeron sounded

confident. 'Oh yeah,' he said, 'before we turned down-wind I saw him at about one o'clock. Probably behind us now.' Flight 182 lowered its wheels for the landing.

But the Cessna was not behind them. They were still overtaking it – and descending while Boswell and Kazy were climbing. To add to the danger, at 09.00.45 the course of the Cessna had changed for some reason from 070 to 090. It was the final element in the equation.

Witnesses on the ground watched in horror as the Boeing banked slightly to the right, and the startled Cessna pilot pitched nose up as he saw the massive shape coming down on top of him. The propeller of the light plane tore into the right wing of flight 182, doing fatal damage. The time was 09.01.47.

For four long seconds there was no reaction in the cockpit of the stricken 727. Then McFeron said: 'What have we got here?'

'It's bad,' said the flight engineer, and Fox cried, 'We're hit, man, we're hit.'

The last tragic words on the cockpit voice-recorder came at 09.02.04. A single voice said, 'Ma, I love you.'

There were no survivors from either aircraft, and seven people on the ground died as well. The inquest which followed blamed the crew of flight 182 for failing to keep clear of the Cessna and for not telling the controller when they had lost sight of it. But the control procedure which allowed the aircraft to rely on the pilots' eyesight alone when they could easily have been separated by radar also came in for attack. The controller had been playing it by the book, but the book was wrong. Now, a little late, it has been changed.

What makes the San Diego accident all the more tragic and inexplicable is the fact that the airport was equipped with the very latest device to prevent such a thing happening. Known as a conflict alert system, this is a computer which projects an invisible ring five miles in diameter and 2000 feet in height around the radar response of each aircraft. If two rings should touch, indicating that the aircraft are too close to each other for comfort, a warning bell sounds to alert the controller.

The conflict alert system had been commissioned at San Diego some seven weeks before the disaster. It worked. On average the warning bell had gone off thirteen times a day since it had been brought into operation; it sounded again that morning as flight 182 and the Cessna approached their fatal rendezvous. Was it a case of 'cry wolf'? Who knows? There were no FAA rules to tell the controller that he must warn the pilot when the bell rang or indeed that he should do anything at all. Perhaps it is easy to say afterwards that, when rules do not exist, common sense should prevail. On this occasion, for 145 people, there was no afterwards.

The history of air safety is littered with examples of lessons which are only learned after the accident has happened. Indeed, the cynical would say that this is the only way in which they are ever learned. In the case of the conflict alert system, the order for its introduction came after a little contretemps between a Lockheed Tristar of Trans World Airlines and an American Airlines DC10 over Carlton, Michigan, on 26 November 1975. By a curious coincidence, the flight number of the DC10 was also 182.

The DC10 with 179 passengers and thirteen crew on board was flying from San Francisco to Newark, New Jersey, with an intermediate stop at Chicago. Its captain was forty-seven-year-old Guy Eby, a highly experienced pilot with 21,600 flying hours, 670 of them in the DC10. He was to need all his experience before the day was out. Beside him in the right-hand seat sat First Officer David Narins. In age, Narins was only four years Eby's junior, but he was far less experienced, with only about one-third of his captain's flying hours. The veteran on the flight deck was the engineer, fifty-three-year-old Bruce Hopkins, himself a pilot. Together they brought American Airlines flight 182 to Chicago without incident and took off again for their final destination at 18.39 Eastern Standard Time. They were climbing eastbound under the control of Cleveland Air Route Traffic Control Center.

Twenty-four minutes earlier, TWA flight 37, a Lockheed Tristar, had taken off from Philadelphia bound for Los Angeles with 103 passengers and a crew of eleven. It too was under the control of the Cleveland centre, whose radar that evening was manned by Drew Parker, Charles Hewitt and Leroy Wade, all experienced controllers.

The evening of 28 November was a cloudy one over Michigan. Thick, impenetrable clag, with the consistency of old socks, piled high into the atmosphere to over 30,000 feet. At least four airliners were overhead, crews alert in their cockpits, eyes blind to all but their instruments, ears tuned to the guiding voice of the ground controller and the conversation of other pilots on the same frequency. Behind them the passengers sipped their drinks as the cabin staff busied themselves with the dinner trays.

One of the four was United Airlines flight 680, climbing to 33,000 feet, still in cloud and anxious to know when he would break clear. The pilot pressed his transmit button and spoke to Cleveland control. 'Any idea of the tops?' he asked.

'They were at 35 earlier,' replied the controller. 'Just a moment, let me check.'

The controller passed on the query to TWA37, which he knew from its radar transponder was flying at 35,000 feet. 'Well, they are higher than we are,' the Tristar captain said. 'It's hard to say. You can see through it. I'd say it must be at least 37.'

At this point the fourth aircraft in the neighbourhood, American Airlines 26, chipped in to say he was just skimming the tops of the clouds.

'Okay, thank you,' said the Cleveland controller. 'And United 680 that aircraft is at 370.'

It was a casual, informative conversation of the sort that frequently crowds the airwaves. The controller went back to scanning his radar screen, which was linked to the latest Stage A digital radar system. This is a device which processes the raw radar and secondary radar returns from aircraft and presents a 'cleaned up' picture on the controller's screen showing an aircraft's position, its identification number and assigned altitude. In the case of a flight which is climbing, it also shows the actual altitude attained and updates the information every twelve seconds.

Flight 182 was climbing to 37,000 feet and the display showed that it had reached 34,500. Suddenly the controller noticed that 182 was head-on to TWA37, less than four miles away at 35,000 feet. He could not believe his eyes. But was the DC10 really at 34,500 feet or had it already passed through the Tristar's altitude? Because of the twelve-second delay he could not be sure.

Anxiously, he contacted Captain Eby, 'American 182, what is your altitude?'

'Passing through 34,700 at this time. We can see the stars above us but we are still in the area of the clouds.' For Captain Eby this was clearly no more than an extension of the previous conversation. For the controller it was nightmare become reality.

'American 182, descend immediately to 330 (33,000 feet),' he said.

At this point the two wide-bodied jets were one mile apart and closing head-on at around 900 m.p.h. in the cloud. The lives of 306 people, all unknowing, depended on Captain Eby's instant response to the command.

'Descending to 330 at this time,' said the pilot calmly. He reset the autopilot vertical speed control to lower the nose gently to required altitude.

As he did so, he and his crew glimpsed the lights of the Tristar rushing towards them through the gloom. There was only one thing to do: Captain Eby pushed the control column hard away from him and sent the DC10 into a screaming dive.

In the cabin behind where meals and drinks were being served, chaos reigned. Stewardesses and their heavy service trollies were picked up by the invisible hand of negative G and hurled against the ceiling, where they remained pinned. Luckily the seatbelt signs were on, but three passengers who had ignored the sign and one who was in the process of adjusting her belt were plucked from their seats and joined the cabin attendants on the roof.

Seconds later as Captain Eby pulled out of the dive and the negative force was replaced by positive G, bodies and carts came crashing down on top of the other passenger in a shower of plates, food, bottles and glasses. The cabin of flight 182 looked as though it had been struck by a hurricane. Fourteen passengers were injured, three of them seriously, and all ten flight attendants had minor injuries.

A shaken Captain Eby made an emergency landing at Wayne Airport, Detroit, thankful to be alive. As for the TWA Tristar, its crew never even saw the DC10 though it had missed them by less than 100 feet. They were told of the near collision when they arrived in Los Angeles.

Twelve days later, on 8 December 1975, the FAA ordered the installation of conflict alert systems at all air-traffic control centres as soon as possible.

But will increased automation prevent such things happening? It certainly failed to do so at San Diego. At the NTSB inquiry which followed the Michigan affair, during which it was revealed that there had been ten cases of 'indequate separation' at the Cleveland centre alone during 1975, there were warnings that automation can induce complacency.

It emerged at the inquiry that there had been a change-over in controllers only two minutes before the near-disaster. The first controller had apparently become so preoccupied with secondary duties (the chat about the cloud tops) that he had failed to see the impending conflict. Certainly he had made no mention of it when he handed over the position to his colleague, and the latter had no reason to think that he was being saddled with an acute problem.

The N T S B concluded:

Had the controller been working with broad band radar (the old-fashioned variety which merely gives the plan position of the aircraft) he would have been forced to take steps as soon as 182 was handed off to him. He could have stopped it climbing, or made it report at 310 (31,000 feet). However, the automatic altitude readout induced him to rely solely on his own observations of the computer-processed data. He did not consider the possibility that he might become distracted, or the computer might fail.

The Safety Board is concerned that despite the advantages of narrow band radar, the A T C system failed to provide the necessary safeguards and endangered the lives of 306 people. Advances in technology do not necessarily ensure greater reliability and safety. The new conflict alert system will serve its intended purpose only when it is not treated as a substitute for timely proper separation manoeuvres which continue to protect air traffic even when the computer fails.

Based on the high percentage of human failures in the A T C system, the Safety Board believes that as long as the human element is part of the total system an individual's level of competence, the quality of his performance, and his understanding of his primary responsibilities must be given as much managerial attention as the equipment he operates.

I have quoted this NTSB report at length because it contains a real and awful warning which seems to have been ignored. It is simply this: at the end of the day safety in the air depends on people, on the human weaknesses to which we are all prone. No airliner ever killed a passenger until a pilot climbed on board; no radar device, of itself, ever steered one aircraft into another. Until as much time, expertise and money is spent on exploring the vital influence of human factors as is spent on the development of airframes and black boxes, we shall never be rid of the danger. The problem is not confined to the United States. It did not begin with Carlton, Michigan, or end with San Diego. It is with us now. You too could be on flight 182.

Consider the case of the TWA Boeing 727 and US Air Force Sabreliner near Iowa in July 1980. They were vectored towards one another head-on and only failed to collide because the Sabreliner dived and the 727 climbed. The mind boggles at what would have happened if both pilots had decided to take the same evasive action. As it was, the Sabreliner then came close to hitting a Flying Tiger DC8 which was following the TWA flight. The controller involved in this incident had recently been involved in another air miss and was so unnerved by his experience that he simply unplugged his headset and went home. There had been a computer failure some ten minutes before and also problems with a jammed r/t frequency. But in the end it was the human factor which failed.

In both the Michigan and Iowa incidents, quick thinking on the part of the pilots saved the situation. But pilots have also been known to get it wrong, for the acquisition of four gold rings on the sleeve does not confer instant sainthood. Pilots have rows with their wives and worry about their mortgages and their teenage children just like the rest of us. But if they and their passengers are to stay alive, they have to forget such things. It cannot be easy. Who knows what was in the mind of the pilot of a Hughes Air West DC9 when he tried, and failed, to get his aircraft on the runway at Spokane, Washington, on 1 April 1976?

At the back of every pilot's thoughts when he makes his final approach is the possibility that he may have to go round and try again, especially in bad weather. When he reaches the decision height – usually around 300 feet – he must either continue with the landing or else open the throttles, haul up flaps and undercarriage and climb out to make another circuit.

On this particular All Fools' Day at Spokane, the weather was not good. The DC9 was making its approach under instruments and did not tell the tower when it had passed the outer marker. In truth the pilot was not required to do so, but his failure to speak led the tower controller to believe that he was still some way away. There therefore seemed no reason why he should not allow the North West Airlines DC10 standing on the runway to take off.

Up went the DC10, down through the clouds behind it came the DC9. The latter was clearly never going to make it on the runway in time but he kept on coming down. At the last moment, as the DC10 lifted into the air, the DC9 pilot changed his mind and decided to overshoot. He roared across the top of the other aircraft, missing the giant fin by no more than 20 feet, and disappeared back into the murk. The remarks of the other captain have not been recorded.

It was a classic demonstration of what has become known as the 'expectancy phenomenon'.

The reliability of modern aircraft and landing aids is such that pilots have a tendency to try to get the plane on the ground come what may – and controllers expect them to do so. Missed approaches cost time and fuel and cause a good deal of disruption in the flow of traffic. They are not encouraged but sometimes, in the interest of safety, they are essential.

One pilot, writing in an airline safety magazine, summed up the cockpit dilemma:

Should a pilot wish to demonstrate this controller expectancy, just make a missed approach at O'Hare (Chicago) when the weather is below VFR but substantially above minimum, and no one else has made a missed approach. You will rapidly learn that cleared for approach means 'cleared for approach to land' not 'cleared for approach and missed approach'. To further illustrate this phenomenon, next time you are cleared for an approach, ask the controller what he would like you to do should you make a missed approach. You will be greeted with a period of silence. The expectancy phenomenon can be such a strong motivating force that an approach controller can fail to recognize that an aircraft has landed or crashed, as has been the case in several recent accidents.

There is not much comfort in that. If two aircraft are going to collide, it does not make a great deal of difference from the passenger's point of view whether they do so in mid-air or just above the runway. He is likely to be just as dead, which was a fate narrowly avoided by those on board North Central Airlines flight 57 from La Guardia, New York, on 21 June 1978. Flight 57, a DC9, had been cleared by the ground controller to taxi along the active runway prior to turning round and taking off. There had been thunderstorms in the area that day and the controllers were very busy, but that hardly excused what happened next. As he trundled quietly down the middle of the runway, the DC9 pilot saw to his horror that a Cessna Citation business jet was speeding straight towards him on its take-off run. He was like a man caught in the middle of a zebra crossing with a speeding car bearing down; there was nowhere for him to go. He did the only thing he could: slammed on his brakes and switched on his landing lights.

It was the landing lights which saved them all, plus a great deal of skill and daring on the part of the Cessna pilot. He spotted the lights when he was travelling at about 100 knots – almost on the point of take-off. But there was no room to do what the Viscount pilot had done at Leeds and vault over the DC9. Instead he aborted the take-off and swerved off the runway to the left, rejoining it after he had passed the stationary airliner. Luckily there were no obstructions, and the Citation suffered only minor damage. What could have been a carbon copy of the Tenerife disaster fifteen months before had been averted.

The aeroplanes had been under two different controllers: the DC9 under the ground controller responsible for runway movements and the Citation under the approach controller responsible for take-offs and landings. In theory, the ground controller should have asked his colleague if the runway was clear before authorizing the DC9 to move. Indeed, he claimed later to have done so and was backed up the crew coordinator who said he heard the local controller give his approval. The local controller, however, firmly denied hearing the request or granting permission. Was it a genuine mistake, a breakdown in communication, or a criminal error? One thing is certain: the human factor had struck again.

So what do you do when human beings let you down? You invent a machine, of course. In this case it is a device known as VICON, which stands for visual confirmation of voice take-off clearing system. VICON, developed by the airport branch of the US National Aviation Facilities Experimental Centre at Atlantic City (known, inevitably, as NAFEC) involves a set of signal lights at all runway entry points and a control panel in the airport control tower. Once he has issued verbal clearance to the pilot, the controller will push a button and three green lights will begin pulsing. As the aircraft moves on to the runway, it will break a microwave beam which switches the lights off again. If it fails to move, the lights will switch off automatically after 30 seconds.

It sounds splendidly simple, and perhaps it really will prevent happenings like those at Tenerife and La Guardia. On the other hand, there will still be a human finger on the button. . . .

There is no doubt that the control of aircraft movements, especially in the United States, is a complex and hazardous business. Yet the basic rules are simple enough: keep all aircraft far enough apart, and make sure all instructions are understood. To that one might add, for pilots and controllers alike, make sure you know who you are talking to.

That may seem to be a simple statement of the obvious. After all, any schoolchild knows that every aircraft and every controller uses a call sign with which they preface each and every r/t transmission. Yes, indeed they do. Well, mostly. When they don't, the consequences can be alarming.

On 26 August 1979 a Pan American Boeing 747 and another 747 (whose identity I have not been able to uncover) were approaching to land at J.F. Kennedy airport New York. For the sake of clarity in what may become a pretty confusing story, we will call the second 747 'flight X'.

When it was about 15 miles south east of the airport, flight X was ordered to steer 280 degrees and to descend from 7000 to 1500 feet. Just one and a half seconds later, the Pan Am captain told Kennedy approach control that he was 'descending out of 3700 for 2000'. Approach control promptly changed the instructions to flight X, telling him to maintain 3000 feet. So far, so good.

About five seconds later, the controller was on the air again; this time to tell the Pan Am flight that it should keep up its airspeed and maintain 2000 feet. There was a short hesitation, and then the controller amended that to 1500 feet.

Unfortunately, on this occasion the controller had neglected to use the Pan Am call sign. Thinking the instruction was for him, the captain of flight X queried it. But in doing so, he forgot to use his own call sign either.

Now the controller thought he was being answered by Pan Am. Again without using a call sign he responded, 'Keep airspeed up. Fly heading 360. Maintain 1500 to Carnarsie. Keep airspeed up right now.'

The pilot of flight X acknowledged, still without a call sign, 'We are turning 360. We will keep the airspeed as high as we can.'

Satisfied that he had got Pan Am sorted out, the controller then turned his attention to flight X. This time using the proper procedure, he instructed it to turn on to a heading of 250 degrees. There followed a certain degree of confusion in the cockpit. From northwest the unfortunate flight X had been ordered to turn north and then, five seconds later, southwest. To quote the official version, 'There followed a brief exchange between the crew and the controller, because of the supposed illogical heading instructions.' More succinctly, the pilot wanted to know what the hell was going on. To make matters worse, the transponder on board flight X which should have transmitted its height to the controller's radar was not working. He did not know how high it was, though he was soon to find out.

The one thing the controller could see at this stage was that due to the call-sign confusion he now had one 747 (Pan Am) headed north while a second jumbo (flight X) was flying to the southwest on a collision course. They might have been thousands of feet apart vertically, but the controller had a nasty suspicion they were not. And he was right. He warned the Pan Am captain of the situation, but the latter could see nothing in the haze. On hearing that flight X was leaving 2000 feet, the controller at once ordered it to go down to 1500 feet and the Pan Am jumbo to climb to 2500.

It was too late for such an orthodox move. Within moments the Pan Am pilot had spotted flight X bearing straight down on him in the righthand quarter of his windscreen. He heaved back on the control column and banked right, slewing the monster aircraft across the sky. They missed each other – just. And it may be some time before at least one pilot and one controller forget to use a call sign.

3
Three-dimensional chess

'They will tell you we never take risks', said the young air-traffic controller. 'That's nonsense. We take risks every day; it's part of the job. We're playing three-dimensional chess with those guys up there, and we have to make sure we get it right.'

The responsibility in the hands of an air-traffic controller is quite awesome; perhaps greater than that of an individual pilot. The job has none of the glamour of the cockpit. There are no smart uniforms, no gold rings on the sleeve, no lovely stewardesses in attendance or throngs of respectful passengers. Indeed, controllers at Britain's main centre at West Drayton, just north of Heathrow, never even see an aircraft while on duty. They work in a long, rectangular box of a room lined with computer printers and radar displays. The atmosphere is calm, quiet, and almost religious in its intensity.

The life of every passenger depends upon the concentration and judgement of these men, of whose existence most of them are unaware. There have been enough examples in this book already to show what can happen when they fail, and there are more to come.

Why do they do the job? The work is not badly paid – around £13,000 a year for a qualified controller in Britain, and more in the United States – but hardly well enough to compensate for the ulcers. Yet there are as many as 500 candidates for every place available on the Civil Aviation Authority's thirty-four-month training courses.

Masochism is not one of the stated qualifications – but it must help.

The West Drayton controllers handle nearly a million aircraft movements a year, and the number is rising all the time. At Heathrow airport alone – the world's busiest international terminal – the number of landings and take-offs tops 250,000 annually, with a peak flow of 900 aircraft a day and up to 70 in a single hour. On any given day there can be as many as five 'stacks' of aircraft circling the London area waiting their turn to land, with outgoing traffic performing a complex high-speed gavotte on the airways beneath them.

How do they do it? In spite of the complex radar equipment at West Drayton, which draws landline and microwave signals from aerials all over England and labels each flight with its call sign and altitude, the basic tool is still the flight progress strip. This is just a simple piece of card, one inch wide by eight inches long, held in a coloured plastic frame to indicate the direction in which the aircraft is travelling; blue is for westbound, yellow for eastbound. Printed on the strip by the computer is the essential detail for each flight: the number, transponder code, aircraft type, cruising speed, assigned altitude, points of arrival and departure, and estimated times. A strip goes to the controller for each sector – the computer prints out 14 million of them in a year – and as the aircraft flies into and across Britain it is handed over from controller to controller as it comes up to the sector boundaries. The airspace is divided into sectors so designed that the controller can handle the volume of traffic within each one without becoming overloaded. The strips are arranged in sequence on the frame facing the controller.

Controllers claim that by using these strips, they can continue to direct air traffic even if the radar breaks down – though they admit that it might be a bit tricky at peak periods, and one suspects that they would rather not have to try. On 9 February 1981, they were left with no choice. A total power failure blacked out all the West Drayton radar screens. The system coped, to the extent that there were no accidents.

As each captain makes radio contact, a careful check is carried out to ensure that his actual altitude matches that on the card and the automatic read-out from his transponder. If it varies by more than 200 feet either way he will be asked to put matters right fairly quickly; this is an essential element in the technique of separation, which is what keeps aircraft (most of the time) from colliding with each other.

Controllers have no say over the volume of traffic they have to handle. When an aircraft arrives in their sector they have to cope with it even though they may be overloaded, and allow it come no closer than five miles to another flight at the same altitude, or within 1000 feet vertically. Adding to their problems is the fact that aircraft have differing speeds and performance characteristics. There is no point in asking a heavily laden 747 to climb as fast as a short-haul Trident, or in the United States, with its mixed traffic, a light aircraft to fly as fast as a passenger jet. No wonder that controllers sometimes get it wrong.

Hartsfield, Atlanta, is the second busiest airport in the United States. There, on the morning of 8 October 1980, a controller got it monumentally wrong. As a result, within the space of a few minutes no fewer than five aircraft were involved in near collisions.

The sequence began thirty seconds after 8.14 a.m. when flight 565 of Delta Airlines, a Boeing 727, came within 400 yards of an Eastern Airlines Tristar, flight 453, which was arriving in Atlanta from Seattle. One minute later another Eastern flight, number 399, a Boeing 727 flying from Greenville, South Carolina, to Atlanta, was involved in a near miss with a De Havilland Twin Otter of Air South. Simultaneously, the Twin Otter came much too close to the Eastern Tristar. There was relative order for four minutes, and then Delta 565 had a close encounter with another (unidentified) Tristar. That was incident number four. Thirteen seconds later, Eastern 453 and Delta 565 passed each other with a vertical separation of only 500 feet. Still it was not over. Flight 453 was ordered to make a turn which would have put it on a collison course with Eastern 399. Luckily the Tristar pilot saw the danger and rolled out of the turn early. At the same moment the captain of the 727 pushed his throttle levers forward and applied full power to climb out of danger. Everyone survived...somehow. At the time of writing, the investigation into how it all happened is still going on. It may take some sorting out.

It is not too comforting for the passenger to know that a pilot flying in the United States is bound, under FAA rules, to obey the instructions of the controller. In Britain the situation is different: the air-traffic service is only advisory, and the final responsibility lies with the captain. The snag about the American system is that although in theory the controllers are bound by strict rules on such matters as the separation between aircraft, in practice these rules are frequently broken in order to handle the huge volume of traffic.

According to Mike Simon, the national safety officer of the Professional Air Traffic Controllers Organization (to which all US controllers belong), the rules are *never* observed at Chicago's O'Hare airport, which is the busiest in the world. 'The FAA,' he says bitterly, 'merely want the standards in order to protect themselves in case of an accident, while the airlines want to get in as many traffic movements as possible. The controllers have to cope.'

In spite of high pay and improved working conditions, the controllers' lot in the US is not an easy one, at least, not if PATCO is to be believed. It maintains that at 17,000 the service is roughly 3000 under strength, and that no concerted effort is being made by the FAA to start a training programme for the extra 3000 vacancies which will occur through retirement in the next four years. US controllers retire at fifty-five or after twenty-five years of service, but in practice many never get this far. In 1979, for every controller who reached retiring age, eight left the service for medical reasons. Most suffered such stress diseases as heart attacks and ulcers, which says something about the strain involved.

With the widespread introduction of computers, the FAA has cut the number of controllers in recent years and is claiming a productivity increase of nearly twelve per cent. Simon claims that this is a fairy story. 'Computers give a controller more information about the aircraft he is controlling,' he said. 'They do not give him the mental capacity to handle more aircraft at any given time.'

The computers involved are of two types: the ARTS III, which is used for local control work and simply superimposes extra data such as the aircraft's height and identification on the raw radar picture, and the NATS Stage A computer. The former is fairly reliable and well liked by controllers. The latter is neither. The NATS Stage A computer, installed at twenty regional centres in the US, is a device which presents nothing but processed information. In theory this gives the controller a much clearer picture of what is going on in the sky above him by eliminating ground echoes and extraneous information such as from weather conditions. In practice it has been unreliable. When the computer breaks down, which it did (according to PATCO) 6000 times in 1979, the controller is left with primitive radar equipment designed in the Korean War era. He has to turn to another screen and sort out which of the unidentified blips relates to the traffic which he previously had so neatly labelled. This takes time – and nothing is standing still up there. There have been several near collisions in consequence, notably around New York on 2 July, 1980, when the system broke down for two and a half hours during a night-time peak traffic period. On this occasion the FAA denied that there had been any risk to passengers. The controllers, who may have been in a better position to know, disagreed strongly. When a computer does fail, the situation is further complicated by the fact that the controller has no way of knowing whether the failure will last for a few seconds or several hours. This does nothing for his peace of mind.

That is the situation in the United States. Passengers in Britain will be pleased to know that although the West Drayton centre is due to change over to a very similar computerized system to the NATS Stage A during 1981, these hazards will be much diminished. Because the British, in their slow and methodical way, did not jump straight from basic radar to the higher reaches of technology, a breakdown of the new computer will merely let the system revert to its present semi-automated state. And that, says the CAA, is perfectly safe. The new radar is impressive, allowing the controller to take a close and magnified look at any sector where problems may be building up. It will certainly help to control the congested skies, but at the end of the day it will still be the human factor that counts and which, for all the intensive training and close supervision, is still occasionally fallible.

In the American context, PATCO can easily be accused of special pleading on behalf of controllers. Certainly not everyone sees the plight of its members as being quite so dire. Gerry Bruggink, former deputy director of the

National Transportation Safety Board and one of the most respected figures in the world of aviation safety, told me, 'There is probably no group of people who have a better thing going for them than the traffic controllers. I don't say they don't deserve it, but their working conditions have improved considerably and the FAA has been extremely lenient on early retirement. People who cannot hack it (i.e. do the job) are not even asked too many questions. They get a second job opportunity within the Administration and it costs millions of dollars to retrain them. As for medical retirement, I am suspicious by nature. They know exactly what symptoms to show. The FAA is treating the controllers with kid gloves.'

Bruggink, a lean and courteous Dutchman who flew Spitfires during World War II and survived the notorious death railway after capture by the Japanese, now lives in semi-retirement with his wife on 33 acres of unspoiled woodland in Alabama. He is critical of the FAA's failure to produce a back-up for its automated system and the fact that modern controllers are not trained to operate in the old way if the new apparatus goes wrong. 'It really is a horrifying thought that a controller can have a scope full of aircraft and then suddenly has to reconstruct it. What do all those airplanes do in the meantime?' What, indeed?

Bruggink is also strongly opposed to the overloading of the air-traffic system, and thinks the situation at Chicago should never have been allowed to happen. 'It seems that every time we make an improvement in the system we immediately use that improvement to add to its capacity. I think there should be a cut-off point where we say that people can only do so much at a time. Air carriers should take that into consideration and have an equitable distribution of flights into a certain area.'

There is no sign that such a thing is happening, at least not in the United States. The traffic continues to grow and controllers continue to cope – after a fashion. The building of more airports might be a solution but, expense apart, the environmentalists are strongly entrenched.

In Europe, as British holidaymakers who have sat around Heathrow, Gatwick and Luton for hours on end will know, the increasing number of aircraft has led to the imposition of 'flow control'. Flights are not allowed to take off until it is certain they will be able to pass through the complex system of national air-traffic controls and land at their destination without further delay. This saves fuel, and therefore money, for the operators. And since few of the airports in southern Europe have yet got round to fitting approach-control radar, it also makes life safer for the passengers. One day it may even be possible to schedule departures so that aircraft take off when the airlines say they will, but this is no place for dreaming.

British controllers are at least spared the computer-induced agonies of their American counterparts. Automation has not gone so far in Britain, but the coming of Mode C secondary radar, which records the height of an aircraft on the screen through a transponder in the cockpit, has been a major advance in recent years. Remarkably, however, it was only installed at Gatwick in 1980.

There is one other advantage enjoyed by British controllers: each and every one of them is a pilot, trained to at least private pilot licence standard. Although flying a light aircraft is a very different matter from piloting a large jet, the controllers at least have something in common with the men they are directing. When it comes to communication and the mutual trust which must exist, this is highly important. Antagonism between pilots and controllers, which has been known to exist, is bad news for all of us who hope to get down in one piece.

On the other hand, when it comes to gaining actual

experience on the flight deck of an airliner, the Americans have a better deal. The British controllers are only allowed two flights a year by an economy-minded CAA – and they may have to queue for those. US controllers can have up to eight trips on the jump seat each year, but they get them by courtesy of the airlines. Cases of disgruntled controllers giving less than adequate service to an airline which has refused them a trip are not unknown. Which could be hard on the passenger, as well as on the pilot.

Equally important, of course, is familiarity of pilots with what goes on at air-traffic control centres. West Drayton is open to pilots at any hour of the day or night and actively encourages them to come along and discuss their problems. The offer is frequently taken up by Britain's independent airlines, who take organized parties of their flight crews through the centre on a regular basis. The pilots who are never seen there are those from British Airways, though with a base just across the road they would suffer less inconvenience than any. Perhaps those lordly gentlemen feel themselves in no need of instruction concerning the way they are guided through the skies. Let us all hope they are right.

4

The human factor

They never found the passenger from seat 17H. He lies there still, somewhere in the rugged country around Socorro, New Mexico, where he has lain since 2 November 1973. They gave up searching long ago.

Socorro was not where the man from 17H expected to finish his journey. Along with 115 other passengers and twelve crew, he was bound for San Francisco on flight 27, a DC10 operated by National Airlines. Flight 27 was a scheduled trip between Miami and San Francisco stopping along the way at New Orleans, Houston and Las Vegas. Its captain, veteran pilot William R. Broocke, had accumulated 21,853 flying hours in his fifty-four years, 801 of them in the DC10. His first officer, twenty-one years his junior, was Eddie H. Saunders, with 7086 hours of flying under his wings, and 445 of them in the DC10. The third man on the flight deck, who was to play a crucial role, was flight engineer Golden W. Hanks, aged fifty-five, who had more hours' experience in the DC10, at 1252, than the captain and first officer together. In view of what was to happen, this is worth remembering.

So there was flight 27, most modern jet of its day, with a mature and highly experienced crew. Lightly loaded, it soared through the clear skies above New Mexico at 39,000 feet and an indicated air speed of 257 knots.

The DC10 was powered by three General Electric CF-6-60 engines, one under each wing and one in the tail. Numbers one and two had done 4130 hours and 2660 hours respectively. Neither had given any trouble throughout its life and neither had been overhauled. Number three engine, however, beneath the right wing, had been giving National Airlines quite a lot of bother in the 5089 hours it had run since new. It had been removed for inspection, re-installed and then taken off again eight days later for a compressor discharge pressure leak. After repair it was removed again because of lagging performance, and it was found that a vane and a turbine blade had failed. Again it was repaired and put in a different aircraft only to be taken off, modified, and replaced the following day. On 13 September 1973, it was again removed because of turbine damage and combustion failure. It was hung beneath the wing of the DC10 which was to become flight 27 on 23 September.

Like most aircraft of its class, this DC10 was fitted with a sophisticated autothrottle control which can keep the aircraft at a constant speed and helps to conserve fuel. Once he had reached his cruising altitude, Captain Broocke set the device for 257 knots and relaxed. The time was just coming up to 16.40.

It seems that the flight engineer, Golden Hanks, was curious to find out how this modern miracle worked. According to the cockpit voice-recorder examined later, the following conversation took place.

Golden Hanks: 'I wonder, if you pull the number one tach (tachometer) will that . . . autothrottle respond to anything?'

Captain Broocke: 'Gee, I don't know.'

Golden Hanks: 'You want to try it and see?'

Captain Broocke: 'Yeah, let's see.'

Golden Hanks: 'You're on speed right now though.'

Captain Broocke: 'Well, I haven't got it. There it is. I guess it does. Right on the nose.'

This somewhat enigmatic exchange came to a sudden

conclusion. As Captain Broocke said the word 'nose', the sound of an explosion could clearly be heard on the cockpit voice-recorder. As a result of the captain fiddling with the controls, the number three engine had over-speeded, the vanes of its fan assembly had touched the outer casing, and the engine had exploded.

In the passenger cabin behind, the results were catastrophic. A fragment of the disintegrating engine smashed the window beside seat 17H, and there was an instantaneous explosive decompression. Before the accident, the air in the cabin had been at atmospheric pressure 8.7 pounds per square inch greater than the near-vacuum existing outside at 39,000 feet. Now it all tried to rush out of the broken window. The cabin filled with blue-grey smoke.

In his seat beside the window, the passenger from 17H had his lap-strap only loosely fastened. The 8 inches of slack allowed his body to be sucked halfway through the small window opening by the outrushing gale of air and there was a macabre tug-of-war as the passenger in the next seat tried to drag him back. It was no use – the passenger from 17H was expelled from the aircraft and began his long, tumbling fall to earth. The New Mexico state police, using a computer analysis to assess the trajectory of his fall, searched for days but never discovered the body.

Meanwhile, in the cabin oxygen masks were popping out as a hail of loose articles followed the unlucky victim out of the window.

Though the pilot had put the DC10 into an instant dive, passengers were exposed to an altitude of more than 30,000 feet – higher than Mount Everest – for more than a minute. They were above 25,000 feet for more than two minutes. Without oxygen, this exposure is enough to render a human being unconscious.

It was time for the passengers on flight 27 to find out the hard way whether the emergency oxygen equipment, so prettily demonstrated by the stewardesses at the start of every trip, really worked. Some did and some didn't. From the time of the decompression, the delay in the presentation of the oxygen masks ranged from several seconds to more than three minutes. Several flight attendants and some of the passengers had to force open the compartment doors to get at the oxygen apparatus inside. Some leaned towards the masks rather than pulling them out, which meant they would not work. Others stopped using them because they believed the equipment was defective.

At three seat locations the oxygen masks were pulled from their mountings. This was fairly serious because the emergency oxygen system on the DC10 is not supplied from cylinders but works by burning sodium chlorate within the individual units. They get very hot – around 547 degrees Fahrenheit – and there was thus some danger of fire. In the event, seat upholstery was badly scorched and one stewardess suffered a severely burned hand when she tried to pick a unit up.

There was portable oxygen equipment for the cabin crew, but none of them used it. Two passed out before they could reach their own masks, and the others borrowed masks from passengers and took occasional breaths as they moved about the cabin in the heavy smoke, trying to calm the terrified occupants.

The final casualty toll was relatively small. After Captain Broocke had made an emergency landing at Albuquerque, twenty-four passengers were treated for smoke inhalation, ear problems and minor abrasions. Only the man from 17H died. It could have been much worse.

Later, explaining to the investigators what had happened, Captain Broocke said:

The flight engineer and I were speculating about where the autothrottle system gets its various inputs: whether it came, for example, from the tachometer itself, the N1 tachometer, or the tachometer generator. So we set up the aircraft in the autopilot, and in the airspeed autothrottle mode. We allowed the airspeed to stabilize, and then successively pulled the N1 circuit breakers on 1, 2 and 3 engines.

We retained a speed mode on the annunciator. I was satisfied at that point that the pick-up came at some other point than the gauge itself, but to check further I retarded the speed bug on the airspeed indicator slightly. I merely wanted to see if the throttle followed the speed bug. I backed up the speed by approximately five knots and noticed that the throttles were retarding slightly. I reached in and disengaged the autothrottles and turned to the engineer and made some remark to him that I was satisfied with this function. At that point the explosion took place.

The NTSB commented sharply that the crew had a duty 'to conduct the flight in a professional manner, and not to conduct experiments to aircraft systems in which they have not received specific training or instruction'. In other words, pilots should not play with things they do not understand. But how often does the spirit of curiosity get the better of those on the flight deck, and how are you the passenger to know? Best to keep away from windows and keep your seat-belt tightly fastened.

In spite of all this evidence, no disciplinary action was taken against Captain Broocke by the FAA. Why not? Because, say the FAA, 'we could prove no wrongdoing without the use of the cockpit voice recorder. FAA regulations prevent the use of cockpit voice recorder tapes in disciplinary actions, because the recorders are installed to aid in accident investigations, and are not intended for use in detecting or punishing crew error or wrongdoing.'

Now, imagine that you flying across the Atlantic in a jumbo, heading east at 35,000 feet with Newfoundland 80 miles behind you. Suddenly, without warning, everything goes quiet. The four great engines have all stopped dead. The nose pitches down and you are now on board a giant glider, heading inevitably for the cold waves below. It couldn't happen, could it? Oh yes, it could – and has. It happened to a Boeing 747 *en route* from Boston to Heathrow on 21 July 1979.

The flight engineer on board that day had been with the company for many years, most of which he had served on Boeing 707s. After a spell on the Tristar, he had just been transferred to the jumbo fleet and had spent only four hours on the flight deck of a 747.

Though the basic controls on most jet aircraft are similar, they are not always arranged in the same way. For example, the fuel heat switches in the cockpit of a 707 have a safety guard, while those on the 747 do not. There are safety guards, however, on the 747's fuel shut-off valves for each engine.

It was bitterly cold that day at 35,000 feet, and the captain decided it was time to turn on the fuel heaters. The engineer lifted the cover and decisively moved each switch. It was only when he got to number four engine that he realized his mistake: he had pulled the wrong switches and shut off the fuel to every engine. He at once opened the valve, but it was too late. One by one the great turbo-fans spun down and stopped.

The pilot spoke to the engineer in a phrase tactfully translated in the official report as 'What did you do?' Simultaneously he switched over to stand-by power, for without its generators the aircraft was dead. The engineer moved all the engine switches to 'flight start', but this was countermanded by the captain who feared that the batteries would not stand the strain. If they went flat there would not be much point in asking the passengers to get out and give a push.

Cautiously, he ordered the number two engine alone to

be restarted, and this was achieved. With one generator now operating, the remaining engines were restarted without trouble. The 747 levelled out at 27,000 feet and began to climb again.

A simple incident, though potentially fatal, and one which took a long time to unravel. Investigators were puzzled by what could have happened and conducted a lot of fruitless experiments until finally the flight engineer, to his credit, confessed what he had done.

When things go wrong on the flight deck, as in the cases we have looked at, there is rarely any evil intent involved. It is, after all, a matter of the crew's lives as well. The pilot of a British Airways Trident who defied air-traffic control and advice of his co-pilot and landed on the wrong runway at Marseilles in 1979 no doubt thought he knew what he was doing. Luckily, though the runway was under maintenance that day, there was no disaster.

The passengers and crew of a Western Airlines DC10 which tried to land on the wrong runway at Mexico City on 31 October 1979 were not so lucky. Seventy-two were killed and sixteen injured, while another three people were killed on the ground.

Mexico City is not an easy airport for pilots. It lies at an altitude of 7341 feet in a basin between mountains which rise to 13,000 feet to the east and southwest. There are two parallel runways, 23 right and 23 left, of which the latter is the longer and the only one equipped with an instrument-landing system.

An instrument-landing system was essential just before 6 a.m. that day when the Western Airlines flight began to make its final approach. Mexico City is prone to fog, and on the morning of 31 October it was forming fast. Visibility was down to 2 miles and decreasing. One hour later it was zero. Still, given the instrument-landing system there should have been few problems. There was, however, one snag. Runway 23 left was closed for repairs. Incoming flights were supposed to follow the landing system down, and then jink to the right before touching their wheels on 23 right. It was, to say the least, an unorthodox procedure and one of doubtful safety. Last-minute changes of course during a landing approach are not to be recommended.

On this occasion, two things happened to compound the problem: first, the first officer on the DC10 failed to call out any heights to the captain as they came down the glide path – not even the 'decision height' at which the pilot would have to decide whether to land or to go round again. Second, to make the uncertainty worse, the crew were asked by the tower if they could see the high-intensity approach lights at the threshold of runway 23 left. They could not, for the very good reason that the lights had been disconnected during the repair work and were not alight.

The DC10 continued down in darkness on to the wrong runway, and only at the very last moment did the pilot realize his mistake. He attempted to open the throttle and overshoot, but it was too late. The rear fuselage touched the ground and moments later the aircraft hit a lorry, killing the driver and tearing off the right landing wheel and part of the right wing. Then it veered across runway 23 right and struck a building on the north side of the airport, where it was totally destroyed. The tail section broke off, and in this a few passengers survived.

What caused this tragedy: was it pilot error, a fault by the controller, or an absurd piece of air-traffic planning designed to keep the airport open and the revenue flowing without proper regard to safety? Whichever finally takes the blame, one thing is certain: the human factor had struck again.

It had struck earlier at Funchal, Madeira, on 19

November 1977. This time it was a Boeing 727 of the Portuguese airline TAP which came to grief. With 166 passengers and crew on board, the pilot had been cleared for an approach on runway 06. Then the wind changed and he was ordered to land in the opposite direction.

There was a heavy rain shower at the airport, warned control. But perhaps the pilot felt his plans had already been interfered with once too often. 'I am on finals and I intend to land,' he announced. It was his decision. He touched down 2000 feet beyond the runway threshold, which left only 3000 feet of tarmac remaining. It was not enough. The 727 shot off the end of the runway and plunged down a steep bank, where it exploded and burned on impact. In all 119 passengers and six crew were killed; thirty-seven passengers and two crew were seriously injured. And all because a pilot was too impatient to go round again.

Well, we all make mistakes – including the pilot who came within an ace of writing off his Boeing 747 while on a flight to Melbourne in 1976. Flight BA888 was making an instrument approach to runway 15 at Kuala Lumpur, its last stop *en route*, when there was an audible warning from the radio altimeter that they were a little too close to the ground. The captain called for the landing gear to be lowered and 20 degrees of flap, but at that moment one of the landing-gear warning lights became dislodged from its holder and the flight engineer was distracted. Neither he nor the co-pilot heard the call for the flaps to be put down. It is standard cockpit procedure for all orders to be repeated back, but this was not done and the captain did not query it. Without flaps his speed was too fast and the 747 over-shot the runway, went round again and finally landed in the opposite direction.

When they got on the ground, the 122 passengers and crew discovered how near they had been to disaster. There was graphic evidence that not only the aircraft's wheels but also its engines had passed through trees on the approach. Just a few feet lower and the 747 would have been a twisted ball of metal on the wooded hillside.

Although the instrument-landing facilities at Kuala Lumpur are fairly basic they should have posed no problem to a competent pilot. The pilot in question, however, had had only marginally acceptable performance standards both during and after his conversion training on the 747. Are there many like him?

We must assume not, just as most of us would automatically suppose that alcoholism is about the last complaint from which a pilot would ever suffer. The golden rule, 'Twenty-four hours between bottle and throttle', is well known. It is a little worrying, therefore, to learn that in 1973 the FAA, airline medical departments and the US Airline Pilots Association set up a special programme to persuade alcoholic pilots to volunteer for treatment rather than hide their ailment and continue flying. Since then, some 300 alcoholic pilots have been returned to flying duties under the supervision of FAA medical personnel and their fellow pilots. It is good to know they came forward – but what were they doing before, and how many are still embracing the bottle and flying merrily along with us behind them?

One who will never fly again is the American pilot of a Japanese Air Lines DC8 which stopped at Anchorage, Alaska, on its way to Tokyo on 13 January 1977. It was cold in Anchorage that day. At 5.03 a.m. when the DC8 touched down after flying from Moses Lake, Washington, it was very cold indeed. There was ice on the aircraft's wings.

The DC8 was due for a crew change at Anchorage and the relief crew had already been aroused from their hotel beds at about 03.30 that morning. They left by taxi at

04.30 and arrived at the JAL dispatch office a few minutes before the aircraft touched down. The driver who brought them was worried. He noticed that the captain's movements were uncoordinated, his face was flushed and his eyes were glazed. His conversation was garbled and incoherent, his actions were jerky and unstable and he had to steady himself on the cab door when getting out. This was the man about to take charge of a four-jet airliner on a trans-continental flight.

What should the taxi-driver do? He called his dispatcher and reported what he had seen; she in turn telephoned the operation agents for the contract maintenance company to tell them the situation. That was at 05.50. But the agent decided there was nothing to worry about: if the story was true, then surely JAL or the first officer would never allow the flight to take off.

Neither the JAL despatch personnel, however, nor the inbound crew noticed anything unusual about the captain. The despatch briefing proceeded smoothly and the captain and his Japanese first officer and flight engineer were driven out to the waiting jet. The driver of the crew car, a friend of the captain's, said later, 'He was in good condition as far s'aways as I've seen him sometimes.' The crew climbed on board together with two cattle handlers who were looking after the DC8's cargo of prime cows. Fortunately on this occasion there were no human passengers on board.

Take-off was at 06.34.32; the flight did not last long. At 100 feet the ice on the wings was damaging their lifting capacity and the stall warning horn began to sound. The pilot should have lowered the nose to gain more flying speed; instead he pulled back on the stick and the aircraft reared upwards to an angle of 18 degrees. Then it veered to the left and fell out of the sky. All five on board (and the cows) were killed instantly when it struck the ground.

The post-mortem examination showed that the blood alcohol level of the captain was 298 mg. per 100 ml. The legal limit for driving in Alaska (let alone flying) is 100 mg. In Britain it is 80 mg. Assuming that he had had nothing to drink in the last forty-five minutes before boarding the aircraft, the captain must have drunk at least eight one-ounce shots of 100 proof whisky or eight 12-ounce bottles of beer, all within a short time. Such a consumption, according to the US National Safety Council Committee on Alcohol and Drugs, would result in mental confusion and disorientation, dizziness, an exaggerated emotional state, disturbance of sensation, impaired sense, impaired balance, muscular incoordination, staggering gait and slurred speech. Great qualifications to fly an aeroplane, virtually all of which had been seen and reported by the taxi-driver. But then, who would take the word of a taxi-driver against that of a man with four rings on his sleeve? As for the rest of the crew, they must have been blind, terrified of saying anything to offend their captain, or perhaps merely accustomed to his ways. The cows had no say in the matter, and nor would have any human passengers aboard.

It is interesting that in the NTSB assessment of probable causes of this accident eleven reasons are given for the crash of the DC8. The fact that the captain was under the influence of alcohol and neither physically nor mentally capable of conducting the flight appears as number ten on the list.

There was another disaster to a Japanese Air Lines DC8 in 1977, this time of 27 September when the aircraft flew into the same low hill on the approach to runway 15 at Kuala Lumpur that had been narrowly scraped by the 747 fourteen months earlier. The JAL flight was less lucky. Of the seventy-nine on board, twenty-six passengers and eight crew were killed, forty passengers and two crew seriously injured. In yet another lesson learned 'after the event', it was subsequently decided to review the let-down and approach procedures for this runway to increase safety margins.

Perhaps the most notorious accident in the pantheon of human-error mishaps happened near Miami on 29 December 1972, when an Eastern Airlines Tristar simply flew into the ground in the Everglades swamp for no apparent reason. It later transpired that the crew had been so preoccupied with finding out whether their nosewheel landing gear had come down (it had, but the warning light was faulty) that they forgot to keep flying the aeroplane. Five crew and ninety-four passengers were killed; sixty-nine passengers and eight crew survived.

Less famous, but equally odd, was the case of the Boeing 727 of National Airlines which dived into the sea off Pensacola, Florida, on 8 May 1976.

It was, admittedly, a foggy day when flight 193 began its descent into Pensacola over Escambia Bay. The cloud base was down to 400 feet, with visibility a scant 4 miles. Flying under radar surveillance, the crew began to let down through the cloud, and at 1300 feet they were nicely on the glide path. After that, everything went haywire. The rate of descent, which should have been 1000 feet per minute, went up to 1600 feet per minute. The first officer neglected to call out the altitude as he was supposed to do and, at 400 feet, the ground proximity warning system began to blare a warning. It continued to sound for a full eighteen seconds before the crew took any notice, and then they merely switched it off. Even at this stage the captain could have applied power and arrested the descent, but he did nothing except to raise the nose a little. It was not enough. At 9.20 a.m., flight 193 splashed into the waters of Escambia Bay.

As luck would have it, and nothing else could have

averted a total disaster, the sea that day was calm and warm. It was also very shallow, so that the 727 was not completely submerged, and a tug with a barge in tow was on hand to attempt a rescue. Three passengers were drowned, but the rest of the fifty-eight passengers and crew on board survived.

Asked how the accident had happened, the captain later said that he had misread his altimeter. He thought it indicated 1500 feet when in fact it was only 500. Well, some types of altimeter are confusing, but since he had been cleared out of 1500 feet only a minute previously, the explanation was not too convincing.

But pilots sometimes do strange things, and often get away with them. Witness the actions of the captain of another Boeing 727, this time at Tucson on 3 June 1977.

The 727, owned by Continental Airlines, lined up for take-off on runway 21 at Tucson with eighty-four passengers and seven crew on board. Its take-off weight was 137,960 pounds, which meant that it would need a headwind of 3.6 knots to get away safely from the 7000-foot runway.

There was a lot more wind than that. The tower was reporting gusts of up to 50 knots shifting around rapidly in direction, and there was so much dust blowing about that the 727 even had difficulty in taxing to the take-off point. A prudent pilot might have gone back to the ramp and waited for things to calm down. This one, for whatever reason, decided to carry on. As he began his take-off run there was a headwind of more than 40 knots, but at mid-point in the runway there was dead calm. As the 727 tried to lift into the air it was struck by a tailwind of 50 knots. It was more than the aircraft could take. The pilot struggled to gain height, but the plane struck power lines 710 feet beyond the end of the runway and suffered severe damage to its underside. Fuel tanks were ruptured and the wings suffered internally, but somehow the 727 managed to stay in the air. The captain limped around the circuit and returned to make a safe landing, perhaps reflecting that if he had bothered to use the full length of the runway, instead of starting 500 feet from the end, he might have saved himself some trouble. Not to mention a few incipient heart attacks behind him.

Even so, a report later found that if the 727 pilot had known more about the capabilities of his aeroplane, he could still have avoided the incident in spite of his initial mistakes. This is a recurrent theme in accident reports (there are those who believe that the Chicago DC10 could have been saved if the pilot had acted differently when the engine fell off) and a worrying one. Are pilots so conditioned to fly 'by the book' that they cannot react to an emergency situation? Or is the book itself deficient? Both contentions will no doubt be denied, but there have been enough broken aeroplanes and mangled bodies to show that something is wrong somewhere. With the development of the sophisticated simulators on which so much training is now done it should be possible to re-enact a vast range of emergencies, including the grossly improbable as well as the more usual variety. Or perhaps pilots need more training in how to crash successfully. That may sound odd, but many an accident would not have been fatal if the pilot had known more the the gentle art of crashing in one piece. Airport authorities could help too by eliminating obstructions from both ends of the runway.

The National Transportation Safety Board in the United States believes that airline pilots generally have little knowledge of the distance they need to make an overshoot under different conditions of temperature, elevation, velocity, gross weight and loss of power caused by engine failure. If this is so, it is a serious omission. When the chips are down those are precisely the things the pilot needs to know, for all our sakes.

Yet it may well be that when danger seems imminent some sort of emergency mechanism cuts in to override the pilot's normal reasoning taught by experience and training. It forces him instead to get out of the situation rapidly and impulsively – and if he succeeds it will either be by inherent skill or pure chance. Unfortunately neither was on hand at the Harry S. Truman airport in the Virgin Islands on 27 April 1976.

The island of St Thomas is no place for a disaster. Green and lush, surrounded by palm-fringed beaches and studded with gentle mountains, it is a typical Caribbean slice of paradise. American tourists come in their thousands, and the airport runway, jutting out to sea on its foundation of crushed coral, has been extended to take all but the biggest jets. For aircraft that approach over the sea, Thomas must be rather like driving up a cul-de-sac: the hills at the far end of the runway leave little margin for error.

It was late in the holiday season when the Boeing 727 of American Airlines flying from New York began its approach to St Thomas. There were only eighty-eight people on board including the crew.

As the aircraft crossed the runway threshold there was a 30-degree crosswind blowing at 12 knots; not enough to cause embarrassment, but a condition which called for a flap setting of 40 degrees according to the company manual. The pilot in fact was only using 30 degrees of flap, which would have tended to make his landing a little longer and faster on the 4658-foot runway. There was still no cause for concern.

Some 300 yards past the threshold, however, when he was about to touch down, the pilot encountered some turbulence, probably caused by hot air rising from the tarmac. The vertical gust made the 727 float a little and drop a wing; by the time the pilot had corrected and planted his wheels on the runway he was already 2800 feet down its length with less than 2000 feet remaining.

It was not enough for a normal landing, but there was a 500-foot paved over-run for such contingencies and, by extending the wing spoilers and applying maximum reverse thrust and wheel braking, he could have made it. Instead, he decided to take off again and therefore added power, then seconds later changed his mind and tried to stop. By now it was much too late. The 727 shot off the end of the runway, up an embankment, through a chainlink fence, across a road and into a filling station, where it burst into flames. Thirty-five passengers and two cabin crew died. The captain survived.

The accidents and incidents in this chapter have had one thing in common: they need never have happened. Nor is there much sign that anything is being done to ensure that similar events will not happen in future. The sense of complacency and self-satisfaction about safety in the aviation world is stultifying. Gerry Bruggink has put the problem succinctly:

We keep glorifying the benefits and reliability of aviation, with only token recognition of its unforgiving nature when accident headlines contradict our sales talk. This Madison Avenue approach to the promotion of aviation may be the biggest obstacle in the promotion of safety because it condones self-deceit.

How can we correct this situation? How can we ensure that pilots and other key figures lose their ignorance of aviation's pitfalls through controlled exposure rather than by accident? When our collective wisdom is sufficient to prevent most, if not all, aircraft accidents, why are we unable to share this hard-earned wisdom with those who need it? Does each new generation have to re-invent the wheel? Does the modern view favour the development to technological and regulatory solutions to problems that we created by treating blind conformity and pushbutton skills as substitutes for informed judgement and airmanship?

What keeps us from instilling a sense of humility and scepticism in pilots, mechanics and traffic controllers that will prevent the levelling-off of their learning curve when they establish their career status? Why are we pussyfooting when it comes to discussing the reasons why less fortunate colleagues bought the farm? Why don't we use our fancy training facilities to develop a pilot's ability to handle situations that trapped his less fortunate friends? Why can't we accept the fact that to the dead we owe nothing but respect for the lessons they taught us in their premature demise? If this sounds callous, it is only because we do not care to admit that every loss in aviation is an indictment of us all.

5

Anyone care for a spin?

Few airline pilots indulge in aerobatics. Their aircraft are not really built for the sport, and it does tend to upset the stomachs of the paying customers. So, though a couple of barrel rolls and an extended spin may do something to alleviate the boredom of the average flight, it is doubtful whether the eighty-two passengers who boarded a Boeing 727 of Trans World Airlines on 4 April 1979 were expecting that sort of in-flight entertainment. Trusting and innocent, they filed through the domestic departure gate at J.F. Kennedy airport, New York, and fastened their seat belts for flight 841 to Minneapolis, St Paul.

The captain, Harvey Gibson, at forty-four, was a dedicated pilot of vast experience. He had started flying at the age of thirteen and at the start of the flight on 4 April had accumulated 15,710 flying hours. He was qualified to fly the Boeing 727 and 747, the Douglas DC9, the Lockheed Tristar, helicopters and balloons, and he had flown for TWA since 1963 after working his way up from serving as an air-traffic controller in Chicago. Gibson's flight-deck crew were hardly beginners either. First Officer Jess Scott Kennedy, a bespectacled forty-year-old, had served for eight years as a flight engineer and four as a first officer. His total flying time of 10,336 hours included 8348 on the Boeing 727.

The flight engineer was Gary Nelson Banks, aged thirty-seven, who had qualified as an engineer on the 727 nine years previously, and also held a commercial pilot's licence with instrument rating. Though Captain Gibson had only returned to work three weeks previously after suffering a broken ankle and had not flown a 727 for 13 months, there was nothing to suggest that the crew were about to give their passengers anything but a normal ride.

The flight had been planned to take off for Minneapolis at 19.39, the 36,000 pounds of fuel on board giving a gross take-off weight of 145,095 pounds. However, traffic problems caused a delay of three-quarters of an hour and, though number three engine was shut down to conserve fuel for about fifteen minutes, the 727 finally lifted from the runway with about 34,500 pounds of fuel remaining and a gross weight of around 143,500 pounds.

Twenty minutes after take-off the aircraft had reached 35,000 feet but it was butting against headwinds gusting to 110 knots, which were slowing its progress and using more valuable fuel. Captain Gibson wanted to climb to a higher altitude to seek relief from the wind and at 21.24 he contacted Toronto control and asked permission to go up to 39,000 feet. In the meantime, while waiting for the fuel load to diminish sufficiently to make this possible, the crew enjoyed their dinner in the cockpit.

Permission was granted by Toronto and the aircraft began to climb. It reached 39,000 feet at 21.38.44 and the crew reported that flight conditions were clear and smooth. The 727 was flying at Mach 0.80 – an indicated airspeed at that altitude of about 250 knots.

What happened next is a matter of record. What caused it to happen is still a matter for intense speculation. Eighteen months later the NTSB investigation file still remained open. The trouble began with a high-frequency vibration, which quickly intensified. The right wing dipped, the autopilot tried in vain to correct the manoeuvre and when the angle of bank reached 30 degrees Captain Gibson disconnected the automatic controls and began to fly by hand. He cut back the throttles and applied left rudder and left aileron to bring the wings level. The 727 took no notice. Dropping its nose, it continued to roll to the right until it was completely inverted. Then it carried on to complete the barrel roll, and did another one through a full 360 degrees.

Captain Gibson called to his first officer to 'get 'em up', meaning the flight spoilers, which would have the effect of cutting the 727's lift and speed. But Kennedy failed to understand him so he pulled the lever himself. There was no effect. The nose of the 727 dropped even further and it went into a steep spiral dive. It was now completely out of control and the hands of the altimeter were unwinding so rapidly that it was impossible to read.

Back in the cabin, oxygen masks, light units and call buttons began to pop out under the pressure of the G forces. Passengers felt as though their arms were taped to the armrests and their feet nailed to the floor. Men at the back of the cabin began screaming. A woman in the aft lavatory was forced to the floor unable to move. Two rows of passengers were showered with cans of soda water.

One cabin attendant, Carlos Machada, said later, 'I tried to move my hands. I felt like I was dying. The only thing I did was to put my hand together and start praying, saying, "God don't let me die, please." When we were going down I couldn't breathe. I blacked out for a second. The people were really scared. People were asking us "Are we going to die?" Then the captain said everything was under control, and we were going to make an emergency landing.'

'Under control' was a slight exaggeration. On the flight deck things were becoming desperate. They were down to 15,000 feet, more than halfway to the ground, and the airspeed indicator was stuck against maximum. Captain Gibson, who lived in Las Vegas, decided to try one last gamble. He lowered the undercarriage.

The landing gear on a 727 is not supposed to be put down if the aircraft is travelling at more than 270 knots. This one was going a lot faster than that. The wheels came out with the sound of an explosion which further terrified the passengers – and still the dive continued. Through breaks in the cloud the crew could see the lights of cities spinning like wild catherine wheels rushing at them through the windscreen. The altimeter was a blur; the artificial horizon solid black. And then, miraculously, Captain Gibson began to feel sensation coming back to the control column.

He pulled back on the stick and the nose started to rise. Up and up it came until it reached an angle of almost 50 degrees above the horizontal. Now it was a question of whether the wings would stay on, as they were subjected to a force of 5.6G. They were now supporting a weight of almost 332 tons.

Incredibly, the wings did stay on. Mr Boeing builds a tough aeroplane, though the designers could hardly have allowed for a situation like this. From the low point in its dive, less than 7000 feet from final impact, the 727 soared up to 11,000 feet before Captain Gibson was able to level out. He had to use the moon as a reference point.

It was time to assess the damage as they headed for an emergency landing at Metro Wayne county airport, Michigan. The flight engineer reported that one of the hydraulic systems had failed and the aircraft was being severely buffeted. It rolled abruptly to the left when the leading-edge slats were extended and the main landing-gear warning lights showed an unsafe condition. Cautiously, Captain Gibson flew past the control tower at a height of 100 feet while spotlights were shone on the underside of the aircraft to check whether the wheels were down or not. Everything seemed to be in order, and he made a smooth landing.

One of the most extraordinary incidents in the history civil aviation had ended without anyone being killed or seriously injured. But in a sense the mystery was only just beginning. On the ground the crippled 727 looked as though it had just returned from a bombing mission over hostile territory. Whole chunks of the airframe had been torn off. To the swarming investigators it was quickly apparent that the cause of the aerobatic excursion lay in the number seven leading edge slat – a high-lift device used for take-off and landing – which had apparently been extended at a height and speed where such things are never used. The aerodynamic forces exerted by this slat would have been quite sufficient to spin the aircraft to the right. It was when it finally tore away from the wing in the roaring slipstream that control was finally recovered. This chance, and not Captain Gibson's lowering of the under-carriage, had ultimately saved the day. And it was the tearing away of the slat which had disrupted the hydraulic system.

So much was clear. What was very far from clear, and remains so, was what caused the slat to extend in the first place. Captain Gibson swore an affidavit. 'At no time prior to the incident,' he said, 'did I take any action within the cockpit, either intentionally or inadvertently, that would have caused the extension of the leading-edge slats or trailing-edge flaps. Nor did I observe any other crew member take any action within the cockpit, either inten-tional or inadvertent, which would have caused the extension.'

Could it, then, have been a mechanical failure? This was the conclusion of the US Air Line Pilots Association (ALPA) which, for reasons which will become apparent, held its own investigation into the incident. 'We believe,' said its report, 'that pre-existing fatigue, corrosion and component failures within the number seven slat and right outboard aileron mechanisms caused the slat to extend. We further believe that free play in the right outboard aileron played a significant part in the controllability of the aircraft and initiation of the manoeuvre.' ALPA claimed that since 1974 there had been more than 400 service-difficulty reports on slat problems with the 727. These had included broken bolts and mounting brackets, cracked attachment clips and failed actuators, making the slats inoperative or unairworthy. Since the incident, they added, checks had been tightened up and TWA had discovered increased wear on slat tracks and trains, especially in older 727s, though there had been no industry-wide alert. The aircraft involved was actually TWA's oldest 727.

There was certainly circumstantial evidence to support the ALPA view. During the investigation it emerged that something similar had happened before when a 727 owned by a different operator had had its number six and seven slats come out at 25,000 feet and 330 knots. On that occasion the crew had managed to retain control and had retracted the offending slats after slowing down to 230 knots and descending to 20,000 feet.

That seems plain enough, so why should the mystery continue? Leaving aside the all too common fact that it took a near-fatal accident to bring these incidents to light, the explanation seems perfectly plausible. And so it would be but for a number of rather curious things which happened after the emergency landing.

Like every other airliner, flight 841 was equipped with a cockpit voice-recorder, intended to help investigators discover just what was going on in the cockpit prior to any incident or crash that might occur. On this occasion, when investigators removed the tape they found that it had been erased. There were nine minutes of conversation on it, all of which had been recorded after the aircraft had been parked. Of what had been said by Captain Gibson and his crew during and after the incident there was no trace. There was no trace of the crew either by the time the FAA investigators arrived. According to Captain Gibson, who was eventually located in a motel at 1 a.m. the next morning, the TWA chief pilot had instructed them not to speak to the FAA. According to the investigator who did track him down, but failed to find Kennedy and Banks, Captain Gibson insisted that his questioner should not take any notes of the interview.

Kennedy and Banks swore affidavits at Inglewood, California, on 12 April, a week after the incident. Both were asked whether they had erased the cockpit voice-recorder and both denied having touched it. They also denied at this time that either they or Captain Gibson had left the cockpit at any time during the flight.

When he made his own deposition, Captain Gibson was questioned repeatedly about the cockpit voice-recorder.

Question: Did you erase the recorder?

Gibson: Not to my knowledge.

Question: Did anyone erase it?

Gibson: Not to my knowledge. I didn't see anyone erase it.

Question: Do you usually erase the recorder?

Gibson: I usually do, yes. I don't recall erasing it.

Question: Can you erase it in the air?

Gibson: No.

Question: What is required to erase the CVR?

Gibson: The parking brakes have to be set.

Question: How many minutes of recording are there on the CVR before previous contents are erased?

Gibson: Thirty minutes. It was forty-five minutes to an hour (after the incident) before the aircraft was shut down and we got off.

Question: So if the tape had not been bulk-erased at the time of shut-down would there have been anything meaningful on the tape?

Gibson: No, the tape could only have made my other two crew members look good. They did a real good job. All that would have been on the tape would have been the other crew members complying with the check list.

Question: Can you explain why it is your habit and routine to erase cockpit voice recorder data on landing?

Gibson: It is an accepted practice, and as far as I am concerned at the time it was done by everyone. It is done by an awful lot of people. When they put the cockpit voice recorder on the airplane I would say 100 per cent of people always erase it on landing after they park their brakes.

Question: Why do you do it?

Gibson: Because I might say something unkind about some of the people in management, and they might take that tape out and send it someplace.

These answers were of interest in revealing the attitude of many pilots to the cockpit voice recorder. They see it as a spy in the cockpit which can be used against them by management. It cannot, however, be used by the FAA in any disciplinary action against the pilot. In this instance, if the tape on flight 841 would have been automatically rewound to record again over anything said in the cockpit at the time of the incident, what did it matter if it were erased or not? But then, if the tape was erased accidentally, why did the crew not say so? Unless, of course, something was said after the incident, and within thirty minutes of landing, that they did not wish to be made public.

In their seemingly pointless questioning about whether anyone had left the cockpit, the interrogators were trying to discover whether the crew had inadvertently caused the incident themselves. Though leading slats and trailing edge flaps normally extend in unison by working a single lever, it might be possible to put the former out of action by pulling a contact breaker, leaving the trailing edge flaps to operate on their own. This might be done if, for example, the pilot wanted to use a little flap to increase lift, while travelling at a speed too high for the leading edge slats.

In a three-man crew, the contact breaker panel is the engineer's responsibility. If he returned to the cockpit after a brief absence and saw that one breaker had tripped, it would be an automatic reaction to put it back. In the circumstances I have just described, that would have caused the leading edge slats to come out, and it is possible that the added strain, coupled with mechanical wear, might prevent one or more from being retracted. The enquiry failed to reveal any direct evidence that such a thing had happened, though there were some discrepancies in the evidence. Captain Gibson, during his initial interview with the FAA investigator, said that the flight engineer had just returned to his seat after taking the trays back when the incident began. In evidence before an NTSB investigation in Kansas City on 29 January, 1980, he amended this slightly. He said he saw the engineer return to his seat, but did not know where he had been. Gary Banks, however, continued to deny that he had left the cockpit at all. 'I don't believe I did,' he said. Then how were the trays returned to the cabin? 'It seems to me the flight attendants would have come up and got the trays,' Banks replied. Investigation into the case of flight 841 was still continuing at the time of writing, including an intense scientific examination of the erased tape. In the meantime, ALPA has sprung to the defence of the crew. In a statement to the NTSB the pilots' union said: 'It has been alleged during the investigation that the crew, through some unorthodox procedure, inadvertently extended the leading edge slats, recognized their mistake, and took action to retract them. This allegation further assumes that due to pre-existing damage to the number seven slat it did not retract, but went to the fully extended position. The crew members vehemently deny that this happened. TWA undertook a flight test to determine the effect of extending the leading edge slats at the same height and airspeed. According to the pilot of this flight, Captain George Andrew, the aircraft experienced moderate buffet. This statement contradicts any possible extension of other than the number seven slat as the initial onset of this incident.'

Their statement goes on: 'ALPA is concerned that this incident is not limited to a single aircraft on a single airline. Rather it appears to be symptomatic of the fatigue problem that has not been properly addressed by the aircraft industry. Recent emphasis on this ageing problem associated with the older jets throughout the world underlines ALPA's concern.'

We may never know what caused the calamitous dive of flight 841. One thing is certain: the number of ageing airliners in the sky is increasing, and their efficient maintenance must concern us all.

Flight 841 notwithstanding, the leading-edge slat is a fine and splendid thing. Indeed, modern jets would have a hard time getting off the ground without it, as is proved by the occasions when it has failed to work. The most notorious of these, for reasons we will come to later, happened at Nairobi on 20 November 1974.

Lufthansa flight 540/19 was a Boeing 747 *en route* from Frankfurt to Johannesburg with a mixed load of passengers and cargo. Including the crew of seventeen, there were 157 people on board when it made a refuelling stop at Nairobi. During the take-off, the crew felt vibration and buffeting as the aircraft left the ground under the control of the first officer. The captain, suspecting wheel imbalance, raised the landing gear, but there was still a complete lack of acceleration and the co-pilot had to lower the nose to maintain airspeed. This proved to be a mistake. Around 1200 yards from the end of the runway, the rear of the fuselage smacked the ground. As it struck an elevated road 120 yards further on, the aircraft began to break up. Most of it skidded another 350 yards, turning through 180 degrees before it caught fire and was destroyed.

Remarkably, sixty-five passengers and nine crew escaped unharmed. Fifty-five passengers and four crew died in the blaze, and sixteen passengers and four crew were seriously injured.

What had happened was all too simple: the pneumatic system for operating the leading-edge slats had not been switched on, and there was no warning system in the cockpit to alert the crew that a vital part of their take-off configuration was not working. An unfortunate omission in design? Certainly, but the story goes much deeper than that. In the investigation which followed, it was found that there had been eight similar incidents involving 747s flown by other operators, which had never been notified to the FAA (as certifying authority) or to Boeing. Thus a failure of communication, an insistence on secrecy, had cost fifty-nine lives.

But wait, it was worse. Two years previously a Boeing 747 operated by BOAC (later to become British Airways) had encountered the same problem. Luckily the result was not fatal, but the company realized the risk of having no positive warning in the cockpit of a leading-edge slat defect. BOAC decided that, regardless of what the FAA or the manufacturer decided was safe, they would have all their 747 aircraft modified so that the leading-edge slats would be tied into the take-off configuration warning system. Boeing was consulted and the modification was made. At the same time, the Civil Aviation Authority was told, but because BOAC was the only British operator of the 747 at that time the CAA decided to take no further action. The Boeing company was sufficiently impressed to print a description of the BOAC modification, but neglected to pass the information on to any other 747-operator. The FAA knew about the modification but had pooh-poohed the need for it.

Nothing more happened until a few weeks before the Nairobi crash when a meeting of airline safety officers was held in London. At that meeting was Mr John Boulding, then as now safety officer for British Airways, who was approached by his counterpart on the Dutch airline, KLM. KLM, he was told, had recently had a nasty case of a 747 which had taken off without its leading-edge slats extended and had nearly stalled. The airline had approached Boeing, who had then revealed that British Airways had a modification. Boulding naturally passed the information on. But he was uneasy. Why had nothing been done after they had notified the authorities two years before?

Boulding wrote to the CAA, pointing out that nothing seemed to have been done and that the next 747 pilot to take off without his leading-edge slats might not be so lucky. He got no reply. Boulding later met the CAA official concerned, who denied he had ever received the letter. Boulding sent him a copy. Again nothing happened and again the official denied having received it.

It was now two months before the Luftansa crash. This time Boulding sent the letter to the official's private address, fearing that the reorganization going on in the CAA at that time might have led to the post going astray. 'The strange thing was,' he told me later, 'that he said he never got that one either.'

As soon as he heard about the Lufthansa disaster, Boulding suspected the cause. He telephoned the CAA and asked if they had done anything about his warning. They denied ever receiving it. He did not give up and contacted the Department of Trade and Industry which ran what was described as a high-level inquiry. There was no satisfactory answer. The sole upshot was an official letter to aircraft operators saying that it was their responsibility to make sure that their correspondence arrived in the CAA office.

Such are the workings of bureaucracy. Comic – but for the fact that lives are at stake. There is no doubt that had those letters been acted upon (even Post Office lightning does not strike three times in the same place) lives would have been saved. After the Nairobi event, of course, immediate modifications were made to the worldwide fleet of 747s. By then it was a trifle late.

6
Wheels of misfortune?

Take-off and landing are the most critical phases of flight. That is when most of the accidents happen. They are also the moments when to a very large extent your safety depends on a few square inches of rubber in contact with the runway. The state of the tyres beneath you is crucial.

Aircraft tyres have a hard life. Imagine the stresses imposed on the sixteen main wheels of a Boeing 747 as it touches down. They have to carry a weight of up to 276 tons, accelerating from rest to around 120 m.p.h. in a fraction of a second. No wonder they scream and smoke at the moment of impact, and that runway thresholds are black with discarded rubber. At take-off the strains can be even worse. Not only is the weight of the aircraft greater – up to 329 tons for the 747 – but the tyre can be weakened by heat generated while taxiing. Even at speeds of around 35 m.p.h., this heat build-up can be considerable; once it exceeds 250 degrees Fahrenheit the tyre begins to deteriorate in ways which are difficult to detect by normal inspection. The FAA requires that tyres should be able to stand up to three taxiings of seven miles at 35 m.p.h., but there is no stated limit for the distance an aircraft can taxi in operational service.

Once on the runway and accelerating to take-off speed, the tyre faces the problem of centrifugal force. At 100 m.p.h., the outer surface of a tyre 30 inches in diameter is subjected to 500G. This means that each ounce of rubber on the tread suddenly weights the equivalent of 331 pounds. Small wonder that 87 per cent of all rejected take-offs are caused by the failure of tyres, wheels and brakes.

High-speed film taken of aircraft tyres at the moment of lift-off shows that they completely lose their circular shape. The tyre is distorted into a sort of undulating ripple around the rim. At this point it should be clear that aircraft tyres are something special, and so they are. With those speeds, those stresses and those strains involved, the airlines are hardly likely to entrust your life and their expensive aeroplane to re-treads, now are they? Oh yes, they are. There is a much better than even chance that the next airliner you catch will be running on re-treaded tyres. And not tyres that have been re-treaded once, but three, four or five times. On the Boeing 707, up to ten re-treads have been known on a single tyre.

The reason is cost. A new tyre for a Boeing 747 costs $1,000, adding up to $18,000 for a full set which may last for 200 to 300 landings. The equivalent re-tread costs $280.

To be fair, there is a body of opinion which holds that a re-tread tyre is just as safe, or safer, than a new one. This is based on the theory that the carcass will have finished stretching. Though there are more accidents involving re-treads than new tyres, this may be simply because there are more of them in use. All the same, it is interesting to note that the FAA standard laid down for a bursting test on a new tyre is four times normal pressure and for a re-tread it is only three-and-a-half times.

As every motorist knows, there are some things you do not do with tyres, if you value your life. One of them is to put tyres with different characteristics on the same axle. Given the higher speeds and stresses, to say nothing of the lives and dollars at stake, no airline is going to do a silly thing like that, is it? Wrong. They have been known to do just that.

On 1 March 1978, Continental Airlines flight 603 was preparing for take-off at Los Angeles international airport, bound for Honolulu. Most of the 186 passengers were elderly, a blue-rinse tour group on their way to an Hawaiian holiday, with an average age of sixty. There were also two infants on board and a crew of fourteen. Flight 603 was a DC10 wide-bodied jet, which at 430,000 pounds was close to its maximum take-off weight. Because of this, the only available runway was number 6 right, which is 10,285 feet long. Los Angeles has longer runways, but they cross an overpass which is not strong enough to take the weight of a fully laden DC10. Still, there should have been no cause for concern. In dry conditions, runway 6 right provided a safety margin of 850 feet should the pilot have to abort the take-off at the last moment.

Unfortunately, the runway was wet.

There were other factors too which were not on the side of flight 603. Some aircraft, among them the DC10, have an undercarriage canted from the vertical in order to make an allowance for camber on the runway. The effect of this when the aircraft stands on a level surface is to produce a marked difference in the load carried by individual tyres. In the case of flight 603, the difference between the load on the inboard and outboard tyres of the two four-wheel bogies could have been as high as 21,500 pounds. In addition, numbers one and three tyres, mounted on the same axle, had been made by different companies and had different design characteristics. This can also result in one tyre carrying a heavier load than its mate, possibly exceeding the maximum. None of this can have been known to those on board as they trundled smoothly towards the threshold of runway 6R. Least of all could they have known that there were a number of patches on the inside of the re-treaded number two tyre of the left-hand undercarriage, apparently put there to seal leaks when the tyre was manufactured.

At 09.23.57 local time, the DC10 was cleared for take-off. Everything seemed normal as the captain advanced the throttles and sped down the runway, but as he approached the V1 speed of 156 knots – the point at which he had to decide whether to continue or to abort the take-off – there was a loud bang and the left wing dropped slightly. The tread on number two tyre had become detached, possibly because air had leaked under the patches. This threw the entire axle-load on to number one tyre, but this had already been weakened by mismatching and disintegrated instantly. Number five tyre was damaged by debris from the first two, and promptly failed as well.

There were 2000 feet of runway remaining. Though the captain rejected the take-off at once and applied full brakes, it was clear to the crew that they were not going to be able to stop in time. Not only was the runway wet, but braking action was further impaired by a coating of rubber over the last 1500 feet and by the punctured undercarriage which had lost 42 per cent of its stopping power.

None of these contingencies was allowed for in the calculations. FAA regulations concerning V1 speeds and runway lengths were (and still are at the time of writing) calculated on the basis of an engine failure during take-off on a dry runway. The fact that engine failures are now rare but tyre failures and rain are pretty common does not seem to have penetrated the bureaucratic mind.

With the brakes still on the engines roaring in reverse thrust, flight 603 steered to the right to avoid a bank of approach lights and left the runway still travelling at 68 knots. A second later the left main landing gear broke through the concrete, rupturing a fuel tank as the aircraft dropped on its side like a wounded bird. Fire broke out immediately.

Within seconds, the left-hand side of the DC10 was enveloped in flames. One emergency slide was deployed by a stewardess on that side, but burned away before anyone could use it. Two others activated by passengers who pulled the handle on their own initiative suffered the same fate. The right-hand side of the aircraft fared better. Some 120 passengers got away down the first chute and more slid down the second before it too was destroyed by fire. The wind blew the third right-hand chute on top of the wing, but a passenger managed to get it under control and several more escaped before burning fuel sliced it in two like a knife. Slide number four got a few people out but then pulled away from its fastenings and fell to the ground when several passengers piled up at the bottom. Before the evacuation could be completed, all the emergency slides had failed or burned. The last five adults, one of them holding an infant, slid down a rope from the cockpit.

The only fatalities of flight 603 were two passengers who died of smoke inhalation, though twenty-eight passengers and three crew were seriously injured during the escape. Had the airport fire team not been close at hand, the casualties could have been much worse.

There were a lot of lessons to be learned, especially by the FAA. Its failure to set any standards for performance criteria in case of rejected take-offs on wet runways with failed tyres was, and is, a running sore on the body of air safety. British passengers can be reassured that the CAA did set such standards (at least for wet runways) back in 1962.

Then there was the question of tyre standards themselves. In spite of the increasing weight and speed of modern aircraft, the FAA criteria had last been set sixteen years before the accident. Tyre manufacturers had generally exceeded the requirements by about seven per cent and finally, in 1979, the FAA standards were up-graded.

However, since they were only raised to the level already being achieved by the manufacturers, there is no guarantee that tyres will be any safer in consequence.

The emergency slides were also shown as sadly deficient. It is not unusual for a fire to break out after a crash-landing; had no one thought of making fireproof slides? The answer is no – and as far is known, they still have not.

Hindsight indicated that the captain could have taken off safely and returned to make an emergency landing, but it would have been a difficult decision to take at the time. We shall never know what was said in the cockpit of flight 603 at the critical moment because the cockpit voice-recorder was out of action. The tape had broken and had probably been in that state for at least two flights before the accident. The captain had reported the fault to main-tenance, but nothing had been done and he had not re-checked the machine before setting off. Under FAA rules, the aircraft should not have been allowed to take off without this recorder in working order.

There was one final factor which sealed the fate of flight 603: the DC10 did not have all the stopping power which it could have had. In addition to the normal fan reversers, the engines were also fitted with turbine reversers. These, had they been working, would have slowed the giant aircraft to 20 m.p.h. by the time it left the runway and would have greatly reduced the severity of the crash. They were not working: they had been disconnected – as they have been by many operators – because of lack of reliability and maintenance problems. The FAA, in calculating stopping distances, does not allow turbine thrust-reverses to be taken into account, and the airline was thus, officially, doing nothing wrong.

The use of re-tread tyres (those which failed on flight 603 had been re-treaded three times) is staunchly defended by the airlines. Yet it could be a false economy, quite apart from the safety implications. When the tread strips away from a tyre, the rubber flies off at high speed and often damages other parts of the aircraft. In the case of a rear-engined airliner, this can lead to extensive (and expensive) turbine damage, and the loss of an engine on take-off. Re-treads are no longer used on the main wheel assemblies of VC10 aircraft for this very reason: with two engines on each side of the tail, the VC10 would be liable to lose half its power at one stroke. British Airways also stopped using a certain brand of remould tyres on VC10 nosewheels in March 1980 after it was found that they tended to strip. In fact the only policy on the use of re-treads seems to be based on a trial-and-error principle, which is a little odd when you consider what is at stake. For example, after a British Airways BAC111 had shed a tread on take-off from Dusseldorf to Gatwick on 29 June 1979, it was found that the offending tyre was a fifth remould. It was then decided to limit main-gear tyres on the 111 to a maximum of four remoulds.

In May 1977, after a series of re-tread tyre failures over three months that caused damage to its fleet of Boeing 747s, British Airways found that a complete batch of tyres from a certain manufacturer had poor adhesion of the cord to the rubber. The tyres were all taken off for reprocessing to a new specification, but it had taken three months of incidents for anything to be done. Luckily none had been fatal though, if they had been, something might have been done sooner.

In July 1978, after a British Airways 747 had shed the tread on a sixth remould, it was decided that no more than four remoulds on that particular make of tyre would be tolerated in future. And so it goes on. One of the problems is that there is no way short of destructive testing to find out whether a tyre is suitable for re-treading or not. All the same, what is one to make of the case of flight BA71, a Boeing 747 from Shannon to Montreal, which lost a tread from the number eight main wheel assembly on 11 January 1980? This tyre was only a second remould, but when examined it was found to have no fewer than twenty-three repairs – thirteen of them to the casing. Somewhere, something appears to be going very wrong. There seems to be a complete lack of communication within the aviation industry on the question of aircraft tyres. The information is available but, in this sphere as in so many others, no one seems to be anxious to spread it around.

Not even the great and famous are immune from the tyre bogey. Indeed, for the rest of the passengers on board a Boeing 747 which tried to take off from Calgary in the summer of 1978, it was lucky that they had a member of the British royal family up in the first-class compartment. The crew of this flight had already aborted one take-off when a warning light came on at 128 knots, but having found the fault they elected to try again. This involved a total taxiing distance of around seven and a half miles, but the tyres on the 747 are only designed for a maximum continuous taxi of 35,000 feet, including take-off. Because the royal person was on board, the aircraft was followed down the runway by an emergency vehicle on its second take-off run, and the firemen saw smoke coming from the left landing gear. They radioed the pilot and the take-off was aborted at 138 knots – afterwards it was discovered that three of the main-gear tyres had shredded and the remainder were completely deflated, with damage to the landing gear itself. It would have been an interesting landing.

Nor is the danger from tyres at an end when the aircraft

lifts from the runway. On average they are inflated to about 190 pounds per square inch, but this pressure can increase enormously with the temperature generated during taxiing and take-off. When drawn up into the wheel bay, the tyre can become a potential bomb – as happened on a Saudia Tristar on 23 December 1980. There were 290 passengers on board the Middle Eastern tri-jet when it took off from Dhahran for a flight to Karachi. When it made an emergency landing a short time later at Dohan, Qatar, there were 288. The two missing travellers, both of them children, had been sucked out through a 5 foot by 3 foot hole in the fuselage and cabin floor caused when one of the main landing-gear tyres burst at 29,000 feet.

It was not the first time such a thing had happened. In 1976 there were two tyre explosions. In the first, a Boeing 707 of Iran Air had a tyre burst at 27,000 feet, blowing off the doors of the wheel bay. The second incident involved a Boeing 727 of American Airlines, which suffered decompression when a tyre exploded in flight and damaged the floor. Fortunately there were no injuries in either case.

This problem was tackled by British Airways in the 1960s after a serious accident due to the same cause. From that time on the airline ceased using compressed air to inflate tyres and went over to nitrogen charging instead. It proved to be a lot safer. John Boulding describes compressed air as 'a potential killer', but all his efforts to persuade the CAA and the FAA to ban its use and have nitrogen charging made compulsory have been in vain. About half the world's airlines do now use the system on a voluntary basis. Most of them have done so only after they have had a wheel explode in flight.

7

Fire up above

'Ladies and gentlemen, this is your captain speaking. I regret to tell you that the aircraft is on fire, and we are about to make an emergency landing. Now there is absolutely nothing to worry about. I would like you all to remain seated, with your seatbelts fastened, until the aircraft comes to a complete stop, and then leave via the emergency exits. If you haven't already read the leaflet in the seat pocket in front of you, I suggest now would be a good time. Oh, and by the way, you should have ninety seconds to get out.

'Look, I know there are 450 of you back there, and ninety seconds may not seem too long, but it can be done. If it makes you feel any better, I can tell you that when this plane was built they got 450 people out of the factory and sat them down where you're sitting, and then shouted "fire". *They* all got out within ninety seconds, otherwise the FAA would never have given this thing a licence. Okay, so there wasn't any real fire, and maybe they could use all the exits, but they didn't have your motivation, now did they?

'I suppose some of you must be wondering what happens if you don't make it in ninety seconds. Yes, well, I'm glad you asked that question. You may have noticed that there is quite a lot of plastic in this aeroplane, and your seats are filled with polyurethane foam. Now it doesn't burn very easily, but I have to tell you that when it does catch fire it gives off rather a lot of smoke and a few gases. Carbon monoxide, hydrogen cyanide; stuff like that. It does get a bit hot, too. About 1000 degrees Centigrade after two minutes, if you really want to know. So if I were you I'd try to make it in ninety seconds.

'Just a couple of other things you ought to know. About your duty-free purchases: I expect most of you have got bottles of whisky and brandy in the overhead lockers and we'll just have to hope those bottles don't break, won't we, because boy does that stuff burn! And then there are your clothes. I noticed most of you were wearing some when you came on board, which is a bit of a pity, really. There's nothing like a good woollen suit for generating hydrogen cyanide when the fire really gets going.

'Now, if you sit tight I'm going to try to get this thing on the ground without breaking anything. And, er, in case I don't get another opportunity, thank you for flying with —— Airlines.'

Fictional, of course, but those are the odds which face a passenger unlucky enough to be caught in an in-flight fire. Time is the vital factor. If the fire cannot be traced and extinguished by the crew, and fairly quickly at that, the aircraft has to be landed as rapidly as possible. Once on the ground, hopefully intact, evacuation must be immediate and swift before smoke and gas snuff out the lives of all on board. Many have died because they did not get to the emergency exits on time.

There were forty-eight cases of fire in British aircraft in 1978, plus sixty-two instances of fumes or smoke. In 1977 the combined total was 114, and the first half of 1979 saw fifty-one cases. The problem persists. In accidents to US airliners in the ten years between 1965 and 1974, there were 141 cases involving fire – more than one a month. In thirty-eight of these all the occupants were killed; twenty-three had some survivors, twenty-nine had no fatalities but serious injuries, and there were fifty-one in which everyone survived. Altogether, of 7043 passengers and crew, 1848 were killed and 410 injured.

Not included in those figures are the 116 passengers and seven crew of a Boeing 707, whose lives ended in a market garden on the outskirts of Paris on 11 July 1973.

It was a beautiful day as flight 802 of the Brazilian airline Varig began the last stage of its long flight from Rio de Janiero. The weather at Orly airport was so clear that there was no need for the pilot of the Boeing to use his instrument-landing system as he obeyed the instructions of Orly approach control and headed for the downwind leg of the circuit on runway 26. Flight 802 was at 8000 feet and waiting for clearance to descend further. The time was 13.57.

Eighty seconds later, the captain received an alarming report from the cabin staff. There was smoke in the rear section of the cabin. He at once requested an emergency descent and was cleared down to 3000 feet by the controller who hastily rearranged the landing instructions. Instead of making a normal circuit and landing on runway 26, flight 802 was instructed to make a straight-in approach on runway 07, then 22 nautical miles away. Everyone was clear that they had to get the 707 on the ground as soon as possible.

The situation on board was getting rapidly worse. The chief steward reported that passengers were being asphyxiated and, with ten miles to go, the captain could smell smoke in the cockpit and reported 'total fire'. At 14.01.10 he was cleared to 2000 feet and acknowledged the instruction. It was to be the last radio message received from flight 802. For another minute the aircraft's transponder code continued to appear on the Orly radar screen. Then it disappeared.

On the flight deck, the crew put on the oxygen masks and anti-smoke goggles that are kept on all airliners for just such an emergency. The situation in the cabin behind them could only be guessed at.

By now the smoke was so thick that the captain could not even see his instruments, and was compelled to open the side windows in order to glimpse the ground at all. As the 200-knot gale of the slipstream tore at his face, he decided to make a forced landing.

Witnesses on the ground could see a trail of smoke from underneath the rear fuselage as flight 802 headed for the ground. The runway was only three miles away, but it might as well have been on the moon. The pilot lowered the undercarriage and pointed the machine at a stretch of level ground just south of the hamlet of Saulxier. He raised the nose to cut down the speed of impact to a minimum, sliced through a few small fruit trees, vaulted across a road and struck the ground hard on the other side.

In the circumstances it was a masterly forced landing. Though the undercarriage collapsed and the four under-slung engines were ripped away as the 707 careered along the ground, the fuselage was almost undamaged. Half the left wing had gone, but that hardly mattered. The fuel tanks did not ignite, and the only sign of fire as the giant aircraft finally ground to a halt was some smoke coming from the right of the fin root.

The crew began to scramble for safety. Four climbed out of the right-hand cockpit window, four out of the left, one from the front left passenger door and one from the right galley door. Both pilots were seriously injured: one by the branch of a tree which had pierced the front pressure bulkhead during the skid along the ground, and the other by inhaled smoke and gas. The unfortunate passengers stayed where they were.

It was impossible to get them out. Farmers who arrived on the scene within seconds were unable to get into the fuselage, the inside of which had begun to burn so fiercely that, when firemen reached the scene six minutes later, flames had burst through the outer shell. The aircraft was filled with smoke and, through firemen managed to drag four passengers through the front doors, only one survived.

The fire had started in one of the rear toilets. Though the exact cause was never discovered, it was thought to have been an electrical fault or, more probably, careless-ness on the part of a passenger. In spite of all the warning notices, cigarette ends are still sometimes dropped in wastepaper disposal units: incredible, but true. Perhaps a copy of the accident report on flight 802 should be supplied as reading matter in every aircraft toilet.

The importance of the time factor in saving life when an aircraft catches fire was never more clearly illustrated than by the Saudia Tristar which met its end at Riyadh on 19 August 1980.

The Tristar took off from Riyadh at 18.03 that evening carrying Moslem pilgrims bound for Mecca. Altogether there were 301 people on board, including the crew. Seven minutes after take-off, when the flight had covered 40 miles from the airport, a smoke-detector warning was heard in the cockpit. It does not seem to have caused much alarm – it was three minutes before the American flight engineer was sent back to investigate. He found smoke in the rear of the aircraft, apparently coming from one of the cargo holds.

At 18.20, ten minutes after the first warning, the captain decided to turn back. He was urged by the flight engineer to declare an emergency, but his sole reply was 'Huh.' As the giant plane swung on its axis and began heading back to Riyadh, the captain sang softly to himself in Arabic; or perhaps he was praying.

The fire was gaining strength rapidly. Within minutes it had melted the underfloor control cables, putting the number two engine out of action, but still the captain remained calm. The situation behind him, however, was becoming chaotic. At 18.28 there came a cry, 'Fire in the cabin!' and passengers began fighting in the aisles. A stewardess trying to get through to tackle the blaze could not force her way through the struggling pilgrims.

'Make it go faster,' said the flight engineer and at 18.32 the runway came in sight as the captain continued his chant. They touched down four minutes later, and the flight engineer asked whether to order an evacuation. 'Huh,' said the captain once more. He seems to have been a man of few words. As he turned off the runway and stopped on a taxi-track, the tower controllers asked if he needed assistance. 'Stand by,' was the only response.

We shall never know what happened on board the Tristar in the last crucial minutes. No doors opened, no chutes emerged; rescuers rushing to the scene were further hampered by the fact that the engines were left running. At 18.40.30 the tower heard the captain say, 'We are trying to evacuate now.' Then there was silence.

It was fully fifteen minutes after the aircraft stopped that rescuers forced open the doors. As they did so, white smoke billowed out and the aircraft burst into flame. The scene inside the cabin was testimony to the horror of the final moments, with bodies piled high against the exits. One stewardess was found under a heap of passengers in the cockpit, where the pilot and first officer were still strapped, dead, in their seats. She had apparently been trying to prevent the passengers breaking through. No one survived.

There were several red herrings during the investigation. These included a claim, later proved false, that evacuation had been delayed because an aircraft of the King's flight wanted to take off. It was also suggested that the fire was caused by one of the passengers using a butane cooking stove, but a later theory attributed the blaze to a leak of hydraulic fluid. This may have rotted electrical insulation, causing a spark that ignited the flammable fluid. However, this explanation, too, was subsequently denied by Lockheed in a letter to *Flight* magazine. Investigations are still going on at the time of writing.

No less shocking was the disaster that overtook another airliner in the Middle East a few months before. A Boeing 707 of Pakistan International Airlines had not long taken off from Jeddah on 25 November 1979 when a stewardess came forward to the cockpit and reported a fire in the rear galley. Smoke was beginning to come into the cabin and on to the flight deck, and the pilot requested permission to return to the airport. In the meantime he sent the flight engineer back to report on the situation and then ordered him to cut off the electrical supply to the galley area. Fifteen minutes later, with the aircraft at 25,000 feet, a mayday transmission was received by the controllers at Jeddah. And then . . . nothing. The 145 passengers, terrified by the choking black smoke which billowed from the rear of the cabin, had rushed towards the cockpit in a vain attempt to escape. The combined weight of this screaming human mass unbalanced the 707, making it impossible for the pilot to control. It went into a long, steep dive from which there was no recovery, and the wreckage was scattered over three square miles of barren mountainside. The eleven crew on board died with the passengers.

Not all aircraft fires are accidental. The danger of a bomb on board still exists, though greatly lessened by improved airport security, and it was an explosive device which accounted for flight 455 of Cubana Airlines on 6 October 1976.

Flight 455 was a DC8 making a stopping trip through the Caribbean islands. It had already called at Georgetown, Guyana, and Port of Spain, Trinidad, when it arrived in Barbados at 16.21. There was a light load of passengers on board – only forty-five – but some of the empty seats were filled by the crew of another Cubana airliner who were due to join their flight at Kingston, Jamaica. In all there were twenty-five crew members on the flight.

The DC8 took off for Kingston at 17.15. Nine minutes later the pilot reported an explosion on board and told the controller he would try to return for an emergency landing. He never made it. The device started an uncontrollable fire that produced toxic gases and along with everyone else on board the pilot was quickly overcome. Eyewitnesses watched helpless as the jet plunged into the sea. They raced to the spot, but there were no survivors. It was not the bomb that took the seventy lives on flight 455; the explosion was survivable. It was the burning plastic upholstery that provided the *coup de grâce*. How many other accidents have there been in which passengers, though otherwise uninjured, have been suffocated before they could escape the flames?

One such disaster happened on the Pacific island of Pago Pago on 30 January 1974.

Captain Leroy A. Peterson, pilot in charge of Pan American flight 806, had only been to Pago Pago once before in his long flying career. At the age of fifty-two he had accumulated 17,414 flying hours, a high proportion of them on the Boeing 707, but his one landing at this airport on American Samoa had been in May 1972. Before he took the trip that was to be his last, Captain Peterson watched a film made by Pan American to refamiliarize himself with the procedures at Pago Pago. Such viewings were standard procedure with the company.

Captain Peterson had not been very well. From 5 September the previous year until 15 January he had been off flying duties for medical reasons. Once the company

medical department had passed him fit, he underwent
simulator training before getting back in the cockpit and
passed with flying colours. He was feeling fine when on 22
January he eased the six-year-old Boeing 707 off the
runway on the start of a long staging trip around the
Pacific.

On the second leg of the trip the following day, the
aircraft called at Pago Pago. Captain Peterson left the
landing to his first officer Richard V. Gaines, who had
spent all his 5107 flying hours on the 707. There were no
problems and the aircraft flew on to Auckland. As flight
806, they took off again for Pago Pago on the evening of 30
January.

Flight 806 was a little unusual in that there were four
men on the flight deck. In addition to Peterson and Gaines
there was a third officer, James Phillips, and flight
engineer Gerry W. Green. To look after the ninety-one
passengers on board were six stewardesses: Elizabeth
Givons, Gorda Rupp, Gloria Olsen, Patricia Reilly,
Kinuko Seko and Yvonne Cotte. Before take-off, Captain
Peterson had the aircraft's tanks filled with 117,000
pounds of Jet A1 fuel – kerosene-based and far less inflammable than the old JP4 jet fuel which had been in general
use some years previously. There was more than enough
for the flight: he estimated that the four engines of the 707
would burn off 48,000 pounds by the time they reached
Pago Pago.

The approach to runway 5 at the Samoan airport is
tricky in two respects, especially at night. Aircraft have to
fly over water until about three and a quarter miles from
the threshold, which deprives them of any visual reference; second, there is a hill on the approach path less than
two miles from touchdown. The name of the hill is
Logotala. It is 399 feet high.

However, there are no real problems for the experienced

pilot. Runway 5 itself is 9000 feet long and 150 feet wide, well lit and equipped with an instrument-landing system. It also has a 'visual approach slope indicator' – a pattern of lights which, by changing colour according to the angle at which they are viewed, tell a pilot whether or not he is on the correct glide path.

It was a cloudy night and there was rain over the airport as flight 806 began its final approach. First Officer Gaines spotted the runway lights eight miles away and called out that he had the airfield in sight at 23.40.35. His voice showed no anxiety, no sign that anything was wrong, though it was a little hoarse. That was hardly surprising: Gaines was suffering from laryngitis and for this reason was occupying the jump seat while Phillips took the co-pilot's place on the right-hand side of the cockpit.

Flight 806 sank steadily down the glide path towards the runway threshold. The faint shimmer of the water was replaced by the featureless dark of jungle vegetation as it approached Logotala Hill. But now nature took a hand. The rainstorm over. the airport was sending out strong gusts of wind which, as they struck the landward side of the hill, were deflected upwards. The wind affected the Boeing, increasing its airspeed to 160 knots and forcing it above the glide path. To compensate, Captain Peterson reduced the power setting on the engines, and the aircraft passed over the hill.

So far, so good, but this was Captain Peterson's first I L S approach since he resumed flying after his illness. He aparently failed to recognize that once on the windward side of Logotala, the upward thrust would cease. In fact it did more: it reversed its direction, and the 707 was now being dragged towards the ground. There were twelve seconds during which Captain Peterson could have pushed the throttle levers forward and gained the runway threshold, but they ticked by unheeded. The downdraught had come at the most critical time of the approach manoeuvre, the moment when the pilot transfers his eyes from his instruments to the world outside before touchdown. In the dark conditions that night, Captain Peterson failed to recognize what was happening to his aeroplane.

Just 3865 feet short of the threshold, flight 806 went into the trees. The landing gear, the wingtips and all four engines snapped off like twigs. Then the bottom of the fuselage crashed against a three-foot high lava rock wall.

Yet, incredibly, the fuselage itself remained intact. One of the survivors said later that it felt little more severe than a normal landing and that there was no damage to the interior of the cabin.

In theory, almost everyone could have escaped with no more than a nasty fright. But luck was not on their side. Fed by the remaining fuel from the ruptured tanks, a large fire broke out on the right-hand side of the aircraft. A passenger tried to open an over-wing exit on that side, then closed it hastily as flames came gusting in.

A few, a very few, escaped through the corresponding exit on the left-hand side. All were seriously injured. Inside the cabin, rapidly filling with smoke, chaos reigned. Passengers dashed to front and rear of the aircraft searching desperately for a way out, but at neither end were the doors opened. Perhaps they were jammed by the crash, or perhaps the crush of bodies made it impossible for them to be wrenched clear. At all events, when help reached the spot some fourteen minutes later, eighty-six passengers and ten members of the crew were dead. Only five passengers survived. The third officer suffered severe injuries and burns and died nine days later.

It may be that if the passengers had listened more closely to the safety briefing on take-off, if they had read that boring leaflet in the seat pocket in front of them, they would have known that they should make for the nearest exit and not try to get out the way they had come in. The survivors said later that they had done just that.

Even so, it is one thing to remember what you are told in the atmosphere of calm tension before take-off; quite another to put into practice in the confusion and terror of a forced landing. Witness the problems which faced the 142 passengers of a Swissair DC8 which overran the runway when landing at Athens on 7 October 1979.

The DC8 was on its way from Geneva to Peking, with Athens as the first stop. For some reason which is not yet clear, Captain Fritz Schmutz landed too far down the runway to be able to stop, and the aircraft careered off the tarmac, across a perimeter road and down a twelve-foot bank. There had been no warning for the passengers, and the sudden stop produced devastating effects. The overhead luggage racks collapsed, showering those underneath with their contents and effectively blocking most of the emergency exits. In any case, these could no longer be seen, because all the lights had gone out at the same moment. The only illumination came from the flames that erupted from the wing sections on either side of the fuselage. To make visibility worse, and the danger more acute, the cabin began to fill with the inevitable black smoke.

In such circumstances it must take the passenger vital seconds to understand what has happened, let alone take a rational decision on what to do. The secure world of his comfortable seat, isolated from life in that peculiar time-less capsule of commercial flight, has been torn apart. He may be numbed and frozen by shock, or precipitated into instant panic. In either case, he is in no fit state to take the calm and rapid action necessary to save his own life. Even if he does keep cool, there is no guarantee that the desperation of others will not kill him.

On this occasion, incredibly, there was no panic.

Though the emergency slide at the front door failed to operate, forcing the survivors to leap ten feet to the ground, 128 survived – ninety-two without serious injury. It is thought that the fourteen who died made the mistake of heading for the rear exit, where the fire was most fierce, and were unable to get back to the front of the aircraft before being overcome by smoke and gas.

Where fire is concerned, there are clearly two important aspects to the saving of lives. The first is to prevent the fire breaking out in the first place, or to extinguish it rapidly at source; the second is to give passengers adequate time to escape. Time and time again, as we have seen in this chapter, it has not been fire which kills but the smoke and lethal gases. Ninety seconds is not enough – in the Swissair crash it took the survivors four minutes to get out; had the fire been inside the fuselage and ignited one piece of plastic, they would never have made it.

The nub of the problem is that in every other respect the plastics used for cabin furnishings are ideally suited for the purpose. They are light, attractive, easily formed and, above all, they are relatively cheap. This is especially true of the plastic foam used for upholstery. There is no shortage of research going on, and new materials have been invented which would be virtually fireproof. However, they are much more expensive. Another possible solution would be to encase the existing foam in totally fireproof coverings. Such materials exist, but in addition to the extra cost there is a question mark over the comfort they would provide.

The scale of the problem is huge, with something like 8000 airliners in current service. Clearly to refurbish them all would be enormously expensive, especially at a time when many airlines are feeling the financial pinch of recession. The costs involved would inevitably push up the price of fares. Would passengers be prepared to pay more for extra safey? What is the price of a life? The one thing certain is that the question will never be put to the fare-paying public in those terms, because to do so would be to admit that things do sometimes go wrong in the air and that aircraft do catch fire. And that would never do.

Some progress is being made. In the US, where until recently aircraft built in the 1960s were allowed to be equipped under flammability regulations dating back to 1948, the FAA is developing a 'combined hazard index' for cabin materials. This will include flammability, heat, smoke and toxicity characteristics of materials.

The FAA conversion to this is very recent. As late as spring 1979 the chairman of the NTSB, James B. King, testified before a congressional committee on air transport crash-worthiness and urged the adoption of new cabin furnishing materials. Staff witnesses from the FAA testi-fied that his evidence was nonsense and technically inadequate. Four months later, however the then FAA Administrator, Langhorne Bond, had done a complete U-turn. The reason was interesting. King's testimony had described an imaginary scenario of what might happen if an in-flight fire at altitude produced large quantities of toxic gas through the ignition of cabin furnishings. The FAA had argued that the only thing which mattered was to control the fuel.

Then came the crash at Jeddah. It turned out to be an enactment of the very incident that King had imagined. 'Since Jeddah,' King told me with dry satisfaction, 'Mr Bond has been very supportive of our suggestion.'

King, a large and charismatic former public relations man, had been fighting his corner hard since being appointed by the Carter administration (as head of appointments at the White House he could virtually choose his own job) and put crash-survival high on his list of priorities. His plan for dealing with the cabin furnishing problem was to insist that when aircraft go back to the factory for interior refurbishing, which most eventually do, the new materials should be used. It would take a long time, but it may be the only practical solution. He says, 'I would like to buy for the public the ninety seconds or two minutes to evacuate. I don't believe that ninety seconds is realistic but since that is the standard I will live with that. I don't want products used in the cabin which give all their smoke and toxicity in the first ninety seconds. I want to buy some time. The present problem is that the stuff that is in there gives you your biggest shot up front.'

There is nothing new about an improvement in air safety standards being inspired by a major disaster. Indeed, it is the rule rather than the exception. John Boulding, chief safety officer of British Airways, puts the position cynically and clearly. 'We often get quite a lot of resistance in our own company to making modifications because the accountants say "nothing has actually happened, so why spend the money?" But if you go to them after you have lost a £4 million aircraft, it looks to them like a fair deal.' If that is the attitude of one of the world's major airlines, with a justifiably proud safety record, the behaviour of smaller operators is best left to the imagination. Though with a Boeing 747 now costing up to $68 million, to say nothing of the claims arising from passenger deaths if product liability can be proved, the accountants must be short-sighted to the point of needing white sticks.

The toilet fire which destroyed the Varig 707 in Paris was not a new phenomenon – merely the first time that this type of fire had had such disastrous consequences. British Airways, for instance, had had several serious fires caused by passengers who dropped lighted cigarette ends into the wastepaper containers in the toilets.

The British Airways solution was to design new waste-paper bins which would contain a fire; these had been fitted to all their aircraft by the end of the 1960s. The company told the rest of the airline industry what they had done. No one bothered to follow suit until that day in 1973 when 123 people died in a muddy field outside Paris. 'Then the flurry of activity had to be seen to be believed,' says Boulding. 'All the authorities crowded round to put the toilet areas right, but here again it was after the accident. In the US they developed little fire extinguishers to put in the bins, which made the thing much more expensive than our simple modification.'

If calm in the cabin is important when fire breaks out, in the cockpit it has to be vital. There are things to be done which the pilot will only ignore at this peril – and the peril of us all. Take the case of the Indian Airlines flight from Bombay to Madras on 12 October 1976. The aircraft concerned was a twin-engined Caravelle jet under the command of Captain K.D. Gupta. Carrying ninety-five passengers and a crew of six, the plane took off from runway 27 at Bombay just after 1.30 a.m.

During the initial climb, the right engine began to fail when the compressor casing cracked after a disc failure. A fuel line was broken and within seconds the engine was on fire. Captain Gupta took an immediate decision: he would turn round through 180 degrees and attempt to make an emergency single-engine landing on the same runway in the opposite direction. There was nothing wrong with that. What he failed to do, however, was to act on the emergency checklist which lays down what the crew should do in such a situation. An Indian High Court judge at the subsequent inquiry remarked that Captain Gupta seemed 'blissfully ignorant' of the importance of the list. As a result, the fuel booster pump remained on, and so did the fuel feed valve and the shut-off cocks for the fuel tank and hydraulic reservoirs. All should have been closed. What Captain Gupta was doing was to feed a raging fire with kerosene. As the Caravelle made its final approach, witnesses saw uncontrolled flames enveloping the fuselage and burning balls of molten metal falling away. The heat burst both the hydraulic reservoirs, causing loss of control to the elevators, and the aircraft nose-dived into the ground from a height of 1000 feet. From the start of the emergency to the final impact had taken a mere 180 seconds. For those on board there was no hope whatever; everyone was killed instantly.

It was a human failing; passengers have them too. The incident which happened on the Caribbean island of Barbados on 28 December 1978 might even be considered funny if the potential for tragedy had not been so serious.

British Airways flight 251, a Boeing 747 with 296 passengers on board, had just got in from Antigua that afternoon. In a quick turn-round operation, the passengers were coming off as the fuel was going on, and the refuelling tanker had connected two hoses to the aircraft couplings under the right wing. As the fuel began to flow into the jumbo's tanks, one of the connections came adrift and kerosene spurted everywhere. Though the supervisor on the tanker cut off the flow immediately, he was too late stop the escape of more than 70 gallons through the high-pressure pipe, and the spilled fuel caught fire immediately.

The flight crew were still in their seats and the captain ordered the aircraft to be evacuated. Out popped the emergency slides. The passengers began to slither down. But they were damned if they were going to leave behind their hand baggage and the duty-free drink bought at Heathrow that morning. The hard-pressed stewardesses did their best to relieve them of the loot as they despatched them down the slides, but some would not be separated from their booze. Soon the bottoms of the slides were piled high with broken glass and reeking with good Scotch (which luckily did not catch fire) as the survivors continued to rocket down the chutes. Eleven passengers sustained minor injuries in the passage, though the location of their wounds is not recorded.

It really is remarkable that we should put a few pounds' worth of alcohol above the lives of ourselves and others. Apart from the danger of injury from broken glass, if the liquor had ignited the slides would have burned, and the whole evacuation could have been jeopardized. Instead of a few cuts and bruises and a damaged aeroplane, there could have been a heavy toll of deaths.

It is even more remarkable that the present system of duty-free shops provides an actual incentive to carry a major fire risk on aircraft. There seems no logical reason why passengers should not be able to purchase duty-free goods on arrival instead of departure. This would not only cut the fire and accident hazard but by saving the weight carried it would also economize on fuel – something the airlines are very keen on at present. Common sense? Then why is it not done? I can tell you: because two powerful bodies oppose the idea. One is the International Air Transport Association (IATA) and the other is Her Majesty's Department of Customs and Excise.

The reason for the excise men's objection is worth quoting as one of the loonier examples of bureaucratic double-think. 'Access to duty-free facilities on arrival,' they claim, 'would create privilege which is unjustified on social or political grounds, and would discriminate against members of the public who cannot travel internationally.'

To take the second part of the argument first: since international travellers already have the right to make duty-free purchases on their way out, what possible extra privilege would they gain by being allowed to buy the goods on arrival instead? As for 'social or political grounds', surely safety is social and fuel economy is political?

The IATA objection, made when the proposal was put to the organization in 1972, is much easier to understand. The fact is that many airlines make a great deal of money from duty-free sales on their aircraft and from the operation of their own duty-free shops. They have no wish to see the present system altered, especially since returning holiday-makers tend to be poorer than those who are setting off; the size of their retail mark-up is directed at the latter rather than the former.

8
Fill her up – please!

Jet fuel is expensive, and becoming more so by the minute. Once upon a time it hardly mattered how much fuel an aircraft used in getting to its destination: in 1973 fuel represented only fourteen per cent of the average airline's operating costs – today the figure is thirty per cent and rising. There is therefore a huge incentive to cut the bill wherever possible, but from a safety point of view this is a double-edged sword.

On the the credit side, because aerodynamic cleanliness can have such a dramatic effect on fuel consumption, maintenance departments have become much more eagle-eyed in looking for dents and gaps and leaks in the pressure hull that can cause drag. In looking more closely at an aircraft, they are also much more likely to find minor flaws before they develop into major problems. Safety is enhanced, albeit accidentally, by the close watch kept on aircraft in the fleet that drink more fuel than others. In seeking the fault which costs the company money, they may well find one which could have cost your life.

The development of new and more efficient engines has received a colossal boost from rising fuel costs, to the extent that the US airline fleet, while increasing its traffic by almost 50 per cent in the last ten years, is still using the same amount of fuel that it did in 1969. There has been an incentive to replace the noisy and thirsty old turbo-jets with the modern, economical, and quieter turbo-fan engines. New for old must be good for safety.

There is, however, another side to the balance sheet. The fuel consumption of an aircraft is determined by a wide range of factors. It will vary according to the speed (many airliners now cruise more slowly than they used to), the height and the weight of the aircraft. It is also affected by air-traffic control. Evidently, a jet which is cleared down from its cruising altitude for a straight-in approach at its destination will use less fuel than one which has to hold its position in a stack and let down in stages. There is therefore pressure on air-traffic controllers to clean up their procedures – which might be beneficial – and to reduce separation between aircraft – which is potentially hazardous. It is impossible to quantify how many near collisions in recent years have come about because of such pressures, particularly since the controllers involved may not have been conscious of them at the time.

The problem of weight is more easily identifiable. It costs fuel to carry fuel. One operator has calculated that by carrrying 1000 kilograms less reserve fuel across the Atlantic the amount actually used will be reduced by 300 kilograms. Another estimate concludes that if airliners reduced their reserve flying time by fifteen minutes, they would save one per cent of their fuel costs annually. That may not sound much but, with the cost of jet fuel up by a factor of ten in the past decade and still rising, it is more than enough to give the accountants pause for thought. Such thoughts are highly dangerous. Quite simply, when aircraft run out of fuel they fall out of the sky – and the factors which can cause a flight to be longer than estimated are legion, and often unpredictable.

Needless to say, no airline in its right mind is going to proclaim in public a policy of cutting down on its safety fuel reserves, but there is no shortage of indications that they are thinking seriously about the whole question of weight. American Airlines, for instance, is making a number of changes to its aircraft that are expected to save remarkable amounts of fuel. New, lighter coffee-makers will save 100,000 gallons a year; lighter seats for the 727 fleet, 1,000,000 gallons; eliminating the cosmetic lining in the rear stairway, 377,000 gallons; new fibreglass buffets, 2,500,000 gallons; new-design thrust-reversers, 1,740,000 gallons; and elimination of an extra cargo door, 300,000 gallons. Restrictions on drinking water will reduce aircraft weight by 8.33 pounds for each gallon saved. Those minor items alone will mean a saving to American Airlines of more than $6,000,000 a year, which will give you some idea of the pressures put on pilots to keep down consumption.

It is the responsibility of the captain on each individual flight to decide how much fuel he needs and how much reserve he will carry over and above the amount required by official regulations. Pilots have told me that although they never do, and probably never will, receive specific instructions to carry less, they feel under constant pressure to do so. Such persuasion may be as obvious as a barrage of company circulars through the letter-box or as subtle as the grimace on the face of the despatcher when he reads the amount of fuel required on the flight plan. Most pilots, being an independent lot and well aware that their own necks are at stake as well as those of their passengers, will stand firm and put safety first. But how are you to know when you happen to be flying with one who wants to curry favour with the company accountant?

It may be coincidence, if you believe in coincidences, but the number of fuel-related incidents and accidents has certainly gone up in recent years.

In Britain, 17 July 1980, a turbo-prop Viscount owned by the small independent operator Alidair made an emergency landing near the Devon village of Ottery St Mary when its tanks ran dry on a flight from Santander,

Spain, to Exeter. Exactly why this happened is something of a mystery. The Viscount, piloted by Captain Geoffrey Whittaker, was making its second trip on the route that day, having returned to pick up fifty-eight tourists who had been stranded when the engine of their ship broke down. The aircraft had, apparently, picked up its full quota of fuel in Santander, including the proper reserve.

Yet when Captain Whittaker began his descent into Exeter the fuel warning lights came on and shortly afterwards his engines cut out. In an impressive display of airmanship he selected a suitable field and put the Viscount down without major damage, although a wing sheared off when it struck a tree. All the passengers and the four crew survived with only minor injuries. In a heavier, faster jet the ending might have been different. Subsequent investigation showed there was no fuel whatever left in the tanks. Had they sprung a leak, or had there never been sufficient fuel for the flight in the first place? The fuel gauges on the Viscount were known to be faulty. Only one thing is clear: the accident should never have happened. But it did.

For the United Airlines DC8 which ran out of fuel at Portland, Oregon, on 28 December 1978 the outcome was less fortunate.

Flight 173 had flown westward from New York, stopping *en route* at Denver on its way to Portland. When it took off again from Denver at 14.47 for the two-and-a-half-hour final leg of the flight there were eight crew members on board and 181 passengers, including six small children. The estimated amount of fuel to be used was 31,900 pounds, in addition to which the FAA regulations specified that fuel should be carried for an extra forty-five minutes' flying time. United Airlines practice was to provide a further twenty minutes' worth of fuel as an extra precaution so when flight 173 lined up for take-off there was 46,700 pounds of kerosene in the tanks. It should have been more than enough.

At 17.05, ten minutes before they were due at their destination, the captain called Portland approach control and announced that he was at 10,000 feet and slowing down. He was cleared to maintain his heading for a visual approach to runway 28 and in due course reported the field in sight. Down went the flaps and undercarriage, operated by the captain himself because the first officer was flying the aircraft at that time.

Something was not quite right. The main wheels seemed to fall more rapidly than usual on the DC8 and there was a pronounced thump. In the main cabin, as the wheels were lowered, the passengers heard a loud noise and felt a severe jolt. The warning lights in the cockpit confirmed the crew's suspicions: only the nosewheel indicator was showing a friendly green. On the ground, the first indication of trouble came when flight 173 refused to be transferred to the tower frequency by approach control. 'We've got a gear problem,' the pilot reported. 'We'll let you know.' The DC8 was ordered to orbit at 5000 feet until the problem was sorted out.

Round and round they went, while for the next twenty-three minutes the crew did everything they could to ensure that the offending undercarriage was in fact in place. The pilot raised United's office in San Francisco on the company frequency to alert them to the problem. He told them he had 7000 pounds of fuel on board and intended to circle for another fifteen or twenty minutes while the flight attendants prepared the passengers for an emergency evacuation on landing. 'I'm not going to hurry the girls,' he said. 'We've got about 165 people on board. We want to take our time and get everyone ready, then we'll go.' The DC8 continued to circle in a triangular pattern, keeping within twenty miles of the airport.

At 17.46.52 the first officer asked the flight engineer how much fuel they had left and was told 5000 pounds – enough for about twenty-four minutes of flight. According to the manufacturer's manual, the fuel warning lights come on when the tanks are down to this level. Two minutes later they started to blink. Flight 173 was fourteen miles south of the airport, heading away from it on a heading of west-southwest; the crew continued to chat among themselves about the landing gear.

At 17.50 the captain said he would land in fifteen minutes. The flight engineer was alarmed. 'There's not enough,' he said. 'Fifteen minutes is going to run us really low on fuel.' The captain told him to contact the company representative in Portland and say they would land with 4000 pounds of fuel in the tanks. By 17.55 the approach descent checks had been completed. Just under two minutes later the fuel level was down to 4000 pounds, but still the captain did not seem anxious to commit the aircraft to a landing. He sent the flight engineer back to the cabin to see how the passengers were faring. By this time they must have been getting a little anxious. Had they known the state of the fuel gauges they would have been frightened out of their wits.

But nothing was going to disturb the captain's calm. The cockpit voice recorder revealed that at 18.02.10 he was discussing the passengers' attitude towards the emergency with the flight engineer.

Everyone else involved was beginning to twitch a little. 'We've got three on the fuel, and that's it,' said the flight engineer at 18.02.22. A minute later Portland control was asking when the landing approach would begin.

'Well, they're about finished in the cabin,' the captain replied. 'I guess about another three, four, five minutes.' Flight 803 was now 8 miles south of Portland, but heading away again to the southwest. For another two minutes, until 18.06, the captain continued to talk about the under-carriage problem. Running out of fuel seemed to be the last thing on his mind. 'How are you doing?' he asked a stewardess as she came into the cockpit at 18.06.19. She might have asked him the same question. 'Well, I think we're ready,' she replied. Now they were seventeen miles from the airport, close to the furthest point of their triangular orbit.

At 18.06.40 the captain finally made up his mind. 'OK, we're going in now,' he said. 'We should be landing in about five minutes.'

One of the engines stopped.

'I think you just lost number four,' said the first officer.

The captain sounded surprised. 'Why?' he asked, twice.

'Fuel,' said the first officer, succinctly. There was a babble of confusion on the flight deck. The need for action now gripped the captain and at 18.07.02 he radioed Port-land control to ask for immediate clearance to runway 28 left, which was granted. It was the first request for an approach clearance from flight 173 since the landing gear problem had begun almost an hour before.

They had three engines left and 19 miles to go. The pilot thrust on the rudder pedals to counteract the asymetric power, increasing the drag and the fuel consumption of the remaining engines.

'We're going to lose number three in a minute too,' the flight engineer reported. 'It's showing zero.'

'You've got a thousand pounds,' cried the captain. 'You've got to.'

Flight engineer: 'There was five thousand in there, but we lost it.'

'All right,' the captain replied. He knew.

The cross-feed valves were open, the pressure pumps

were on; now they were doing everything they could to nurse the DC8 across those final miles of sky.

At 18.08.45 the first officer mouthed, 'Get this —— on the ground.'

'There's not much more fuel,' replied the flight engineer.

At 18.13.21 the second engine failed.

'They're all going.' The captain sounded despairing. 'We can't make Troutdale, (a small airport just short of Portland).'

'We can't make anything,' said the first officer grimly.

At 18.13.46 the captain ordered the first officer to call 'mayday'. He did so. The controller heard him say, 'The engines are flaming out. We're not going to make the airport.'

It was the last transmission from flight 173. At 18.15 the giant silent bird glided down into a wooded suburb of Portland six miles short of the runway. It cut a swathe of wreckage through the trees 500 yards long and 130 feet wide.

There was no fire; even so, the casualties were incredibly light. Eight passengers, the flight engineer and one flight attendant were killed, with twenty-one passengers and two crew members seriously injured. It could have been much worse. On the other hand, it need never have happened at all.

The blame for the Portland crash was laid squarely on the flight crew. It could hardly have fallen anywhere else. But it is not always the pilot's fault if he runs out of fuel. Like petrol gauges on cars, the fuel indicators on modern aircraft are not always reliable. The pilot of a Boeing 747 which landed at Newark after a flight from Houston on 20 October 1979 still had 3000 pounds on the clock as he touched down, but before he reached the terminal, three of his four engines had failed from fuel starvation. He was one lucky man. Admittedly he had been cutting it fine, but he could hardly have known when he took off with ample reserves that air-traffic control would keep him waiting on top of a weatherbound Kennedy airport for forty-seven minutes before allowing him to divert to Newark. If they or he had known that the fuel gauge was overreading into the bargain, they might have acted otherwise. As it was, a potential major disaster was averted by pure chance and about thirty seconds.

9
The wrath of God

Dark clouds were gathering over Alabama on the afternoon of 4 April 1977. They grew from small beginnings: first a platoon, then a regiment, then an army, as the warm wet winds from the Gulf of Mexico swept inland to soar skywards and condense in the upper atmosphere. Towering and threatening, the anvil heads of the giant cumulonimbi began to knock together, urging each other to greater fury as the bolts of lightning flashed and crashed between them. Rain and hail cascaded from the roiling, boiling towers. The winds revolved, accelerating as they went until they funnelled up into the lowering mass above them. Then, as though satisfied its reinforcement was complete, the army began to march swiftly into Georgia. Within its baggage train raged thirty separate thunderstorms and more than twenty tornadoes. It was not good weather for flying.

On the runway at Huntsville, Alabama, Captain William McKenzie was preparing flight 242 of Southern Airways for the short flight to Atlanta, Georgia. At the age of fifty-four and with 19,380 hours on his log book, McKenzie had finally graduated through the seniority system that rules all pilots' lives to become captain of the DC9 only six weeks before. His first officer, Lyman W. Keele, was twenty years his junior. As is common on the DC9, the crew did not include a flight engineer.

McKenzie and Keele had already flown from Atlanta that afternoon without any trouble. They knew the conditions *en route* and there seemed no point in getting another weather forecast. If there were storms in the region, they must have believed that the weather radar on the DC9 would give them sufficient warning to keep clear. This was unfortunate. At 14.58 that afternoon the weather station at Rome, Georgia, had reported severe thunderstorms to the station's northwest and southwest – right on the track of flight 242. McKenzie and Keele did not know: they had not bothered to ask.

In the cabin behind them were eighty-five passengers, looked after by stewardesses Ann Lemoine and twenty-two-year-old Sandy Ward. Both, especially Miss Ward, who had joined the airline only a few months before, were to be heroines before the day was out.

By the time they reached 14,000 feet, the cockpit crew knew they were in trouble. The storm cells on the weather radar formed a solid barrier. There was no way round. Vicious hail began to strike the aircraft, the sound of its drumming loud on the cockpit voice-recorder; one large hailstone cracked the windscreen of the DC9.

At the Atlanta air-traffic control centre, between 16.07 and 16.08 four attempts were made to contact flight 242. There was no reply. Then, at 16.08.42, they heard the captain's voice telling them to stand by.

'Roger,' replied the controller. 'Maintain 15,000 if you understand me. Maintain 15,000.'

McKenzie's response carried a tinge of desperation. 'We are trying to get it up there,' he said. 'We just got our windscreen busted.'

At 16.09.36 McKenzie reported that his left engine had cut out. Atlanta acknowledged. They had just lost the transponder return from flight 242 in the radar clutter caused by the thunderstorm, but cleared the aircraft to descend to 13,000 feet.

Twenty-nine seconds later the DC9's other engine

failed. Like its companion, it had been swamped by the sheer volume of water in the storm. Now flight 242 was nothing but a glider with one way to go.

In the sudden quiet of the passenger cabin, broken only the drumming hail, the occupants must have known that there was something seriously wrong, but they had no information from the cockpit. McKenzie and Keele had their hands full. They were over Rome, Georgia, with the nearest runway at Dobbins air force base 33 miles behind them. As they declared an emergency, Atlanta approach control began to steer them towards their one hope of a safe landing. Keele, who was familiar with the approach to Dobbins, took over the controls while McKenzie struggled vainly to re-start the engines.

The DC9 was coming down fast. Three minutes after the failure of the second engine they had lost half their height and were down to 7000 feet.

At 16.14.24 McKenzie radioed approach control. 'All right, listen. We have lost both engines. I can't tell you the implications of this; we've only got two engines. How far is Dobbins now?'

'19 miles,' came the reply. Flight 242 was at 5800 feet, dropping at 1200 feet per minute and flying at 200 knots.

At 16.15.46 approach control reported them 17 miles west of the airfield. 'I don't know whether we can make that or not,' McKenzie said. 'Is there any airport between our position and Dobbins?'

'No, sir, closest airport is Dobbins,' the controller replied. Then he thought again. There was Cartersville – not much closer, but a little. It lay ten miles to the north, a small airport with only a 3200-foot runway, but this was a case of any old port in a storm; literally.

Captain McKenzie decided to try it. Twenty seconds later, however, he had clearly decided that it was no use. The DC9 could not glide that far. 'I'm picking out a clear field,' he told Keele.

The first officer disagreed. 'Bill,' he said, 'you've got to find me a highway.'

The argument was crucial. Given a fairly large field without trees or power lines, the DC9 stood a reasonable chance of survival – or at least its passengers did. A road, with the chance of cars and other obstructions, was a more risky proposition. Yet Keele prevailed. He was still flying the aircraft at this point, and the captain's authority seemed to have broken down.

At 16.17.35 McKenzie spotted a road. 'Right, is that straight?' asked the first officer.

'No,' McKenzie replied.

'We'll have to take it,' Keele said.

The road they had chosen was State Highway 92, which runs through the community of New Hope, Georgia. There was little hope for flight 242. In the cabin, still unaware of what was happening, Sandy Ward suddenly saw trees flashing by outside the windows. 'Grab your ankles!' she cried to the passengers. Terrified, they responded. The left wing struck two trees beside the road, then the right wing did the same. Trees and telegraph poles toppled like skittles as the DC9 touched down on the road, struck an embankment and veered off to the left. Road signs and fences, five cars and a truck were flattened. The mad progress ended in a filling station, which burst into flames as the petrol pumps were smashed by the impact.

Fire had broken out on the DC9 at the first or second bounce. Sandy Ward, in the rear jump seat, watched horrified as a ball of flame swept along the cabin ceiling from front to back. It extended downwards to the tops of the passengers' seats, engulfing them instantly.

For seven long seconds the aircraft careered down the road. When it finally halted it had broken into five sections, the first of them upside down. McKenzie and Keele complete with their seats had been flung from the wreckage. The second stewardess, Ann Lemoine, was left hanging upside down by her seatbelt, miraculously alive. She released herself, landing on the debris of the galley, and ran for help through the gaping hole in the front fuselage.

Sandy Ward was also relatively unharmed, though the buckle on her seatbelt was so hot that she had to protect her hand with her apron to release it. The rear bulkhead door was jammed, so she walked through the diminishing flames to safety before returning to pull injured passengers from the wreckage. Eventually an explosion forced her away.

The final death toll was sixty passengers, two crew and eight people on the ground. Twenty-one passengers, one crew member and one other person were seriously injured; two of them died about a month later.

The weather in the Deep South that day had been quite exceptional. It is fruitless to ask why flight 242 was ever allowed to fly. No doubt the lesson has been learned; it is highly unlikely that your captain will take off without getting the *en route* weather forecast.

The hazards of rain to the airline pilot are not limited to the flooding of engines. A more common, and far more insidious risk, is that of the optical illusion.

The principle is easy enough to understand: the speed of an aircraft through heavy rain has the effect of turning the drops into a sheet of water and, as every schoolchild knows, light is refracted when it passes from air into a denser medium. That is why a swimming pool looks more shallow than it really is. From the cockpit, the effect is to make the horizon seem lower and, therefore, the aircraft to appear higher above the ground than is actually the case. So a pilot approaching a runway in heavy rain is faced with an optical illusion as he lifts his eyes from the instruments to look through the windscreen. He is at a lower altitude than he thinks – and had better make allowance for the fact if he is not to fly into the ground. It has happened.

Though the phenomenon is well known, it is clearly important to know just how strong the illusion is. How much allowance should the pilot make? In May 1973 the McDonnell Douglas Aircraft Corporation completed research on the problem, and the results went into the flight manuals of airlines which operated Douglas equipment. The research had found that the refraction amounted to 5 degrees, which would result in an error of 200 feet at a distance of one nautical mile.

Clearly this was valuable information for captains. They would now know that when they approached a runway in rain and appeared to be 600 feet above the mile-distance threshold, they would in fact be at 400 feet. It could be a life-saver.

But then a strange thing happened. In January 1979, almost six years later, Douglas received a letter from Mr M.C. Van der Stroom, deputy director of operating procedures for the Dutch airline, KLM. KLM, a loyal supporter of the Californian company and one of its best overseas customers, had flown just about every airliner ever built by Douglas. It had naturally received the 1973 report on optical illusions and had incorporated it in the KLM operations manual.

Van der Stroom's letter challenged the Douglas findings. Using a pocket calculator, he said, one of KLM's employees had worked out that the true estimate of height error should have been 531 feet at a distance of one nautical mile. In other words, pilots using the Douglas calculation had since 1973 been assuming that they were

331 feet higher than their true altitude.

The complaint was handled by Mr. G.R. Jansen, director of the Douglas Flight Development Group. Jansen took it seriously and went back to the drawing board. To his consternation, he found that Van der Stroom was quite right. The cause of the mistake, according to Jansen, was a printer's error: the 1973 report should have said '200 feet at *half* a mile'. He promised KLM that a correction would be published.

By this time, however, the original calculations had already acquired the status of holy writ. They were quoted again in an FAA circular on the subject in 1978 which said, 'The apparent error might be as much as 200 feet at a distance of one mile from the runway threshold.'

Illusions being what they are, it is quite impossible to say how many accidents may have been caused, or how many lives lost, through a simple printer's error.

Nor is heavy rain the only factor which can cause a pilot to misjudge his height. A runway which slopes upwards can make him seem too high, one which slopes down, too low. Featureless terrain or an approach over water can give the illusion of being at a greater altitude than is actually the case, while a wider runway than usual can produce the opposite effect.

None the less there have been more than a few accidents since 1973 in which misjudgement of height by a pilot in bad weather on the final approach has been a significant factor. That at Pago Pago, described in Chapter Seven, is one example. Another was the crash of a Douglas DC8 owned by Loftleider, the Icelandic airline, on 15 November 1978. While attempting to land during a thunderstorm at Colombo, Sir Lanka, with a full load of Moslem pilgrims on board, the pilot crashed into a coconut plantation short of the airport. Of the 262 people on board, 203 were killed.

On 19 February 1979, an Air New Zealand Fokker Friendship dived into Auckland harbour only 400 yards from the end of the runway while making an approach during the heaviest rainstorm in the area for 110 years. Luckily there were only four people on board, two of whom survived.

The occupants of a Hawker Siddeley 748 which tried to land in similar conditions at Bombay on 5 August that year were less fortunate. The forty-one passengers and four crew all died when the aircraft hit an 1800-foot hill nine miles from their destination. The margin by which they failed to clear it was 300 feet.

It was a similar story with two crashes in April 1980. In the first, a Boeing 727 of Transbrazil Airlines failed to reach the runway when approaching in a thunderstorm at Floreanpolis, Brazil, killing all but four of the fifty-eight people on board. In the second, all forty passengers and crew of a Thai Airways HS748 lost their lives while landing in a thunderstorm at Bangkok.

Heavy rain and optical illusions apart, thunderstorms are bad news for the airline pilot and his passengers. Low-level turbulence and a phenomenon known as 'wind-shear' can cause loss of control with fatal results – in fact the FAA in an advisory circular of August 1978 told captains specifically not to land or take off in the face of an approaching storm. This advice came too late for those on board Eastern Airlines flight 66 on the afternoon of 24 June 1975. In all, 107 passengers and six crew were killed as the pilot of the Boeing 727 tried to land at New York's Kennedy airport in a thunderstorm.

Should they have made the attempt? Should the runway even have been open for traffic? The subsequent inquiry said it should have been obvious to both crew and traffic controllers that conditions on the approach path were hazardous that day. Yet the urge to get the thing on the ground in the appointed place is strong. Even the passengers, had they been consulted, might have urged the pilot to have a go at landing. They were not consulted, of course. Flight 66 continued on its steady approach to runway 22 left until it met the wind-shear set up by the approaching storm.

Wind-shear consists of a sudden change in wind direction and speed, usually within 500 feet of the ground and often involving wind velocities of up to 50 knots. Such a change has an instant effect on an aircraft, causing it to gain or lose lift and therefore height.

This would matter little at cruising altitude; during landing or take-off it can be critical, and so it proved for flight 66. The Boeing dropped out of the sky, smashing into the runway approach lights and disintegrating. Of those on board, only nine passengers and two of the crew survived the crash, and they were all seriously injured.

A similar wind-shear problem faced Captain Carl Boyer, the pilot of an Allegheny Airlines DC9, when he came in to land at Philadelphia on 23 June 1976. Although there was a thunderstorm passing over the airfield, Boyer was making a visual approach. He was almost at the runway threshold when he realized that he was never going to make it and decided to go round again. It was too late. With the engines blasting at full power and the nose of the aircraft pointing upwards, the DC9 was held in the grip of the wind-shear and continued to descend. It struck the runway tail-first some 4000 feet beyond the threshold and continued to slide for a further 2000 feet. Boyer and his 105 passengers and crew on flight 121 were lucky; they all survived, though eighty-seven passengers and four crew were injured.

It might be thought that a simple caution to pilots would serve to eliminate this particular hazard. Its potential for disaster is well known and though winds may be invisible the thunderstorms which causes them are not. However, the evidence shows that those gods in the cockpit will persist in trusting our lives and their own to sheer luck when landing in storms, and so technology has stepped in. Devices have now been produced in the United States which feed a mini-computer with information on wind speed and direction from sensors at various points around an airport. Any significant change in the wind sets off an alarm in the control tower, and the controller can then alert the pilot to take evasive action.

It sounds like a great deal. How comforting for the passenger to know as he reads this book and glances nervously at the dark clouds lowering over his destination airfield, that the robots are watching over him. There are only a few snags. First, this may not be one of the fifty-eight airports (all in the US) to be equipped with the gadget by the middle of 1981. Second, even if it is, there is no guarantee that the controller will not decide that he is hearing a false alarm and take no action. Third, the pilot is still in charge and may decide that he knows best.

If that seems unduly pessimistic – an almost Luddite approach to the miracles of high technology as applied to aviation safety – you may care to consider the case of the 'ground proximity warning system'.

10

'Pull up, pull up!'

Mountains have been around for a long time. Faith may move them, but there are few recorded cases of it actually doing so. Mountains are a splendid constant feature of our lives; there they are and there they stay, showing a proper reluctance to get up and walk – even for Mohammed. What is more, we know where they are and so do the airlines. They know how high they are and therefore how high they must fly in order to avoid them. They have maps.

All this is a blinding statement of the obvious, so why is it that airliners persist in flying into mountains with sickening regularity?

The only answer, gross incompetence apart, must be that your airline captain is not always as certain of his position as you think he is. For all the sophistication of modern navigation equipment, there are times when he gets lost. This will sound surprising to most passengers, less so to those who have flown themselves. It also makes a nonsense of knowing where the mountain is in the first place.

There are, it is true, fewer close encounters with the high rocks than there used to be. Science has stepped in and produced a device known as the ground proximity warning system, which literally shouts a warning at the wandering pilot. In strident electronic tones it cries, 'Pull up, pull up!' and that is exactly what the pilot must do if he wishes to continue living.

Development if this invaluable item began in 1967, and it was installed by some European operators in 1972. For once the United States was left behind by a technological advance; it was not until 1974, under intense political pressure after a number of nasty accidents, that the FAA required the system to be installed in US airliners. In Britain, the CAA followed suit a year later.

In this instance, the British delay may have been all for the best, though the installation of 2000 units in the US in the space of twelve months did produce a dramatic decrease in what are charmingly known as 'terrain-related accidents'. Unfortunately it also meant that the bugs in the system had not yet been eliminated and many pilots suffered warnings that turned out to be false – in some cases as frequently as once in every ten landing approaches. It was the old story of 'cry wolf' and familiarity with the stentorian shout began to breed contempt and complacency. Some captains also refused to believe the device when it shouted while they were acting in strict accordance with instructions from air-traffic control, showing a touching faith in the men on the ground which was not always justified. As we shall see.

Today, design improvements have all but eliminated the nuisance warnings but there are ominous signs that some pilots still refuse to take the ground proximity warning system seriously. On British Airways flights in the autumn of 1980, such warnings were among the most frequently reported incidents and were on the increase. One BA pilot even disconnected the alarm deliberately when he knew he was about to fly the aircraft in a way which could set it off.

The figures for ground proximity warnings for British-registered aircraft as a whole certainly give no cause for comfort. Between January and June 1979 – the most recent period for which totals can be prised out of the CAA –

there were fifty-nine genuine warnings, each of which represented an aircraft in danger. The figure had gone up from thirty-four in the preceding six months, and from seventeen in the same period of 1978.

Not all these warnings implied that the aircraft was about to crash into a mountain. Most of them were probably caused by too rapid a rate of descent on the landing approach, though that can be no less fatal. The system operates when the gap between the aircraft and the ground diminishes at 4300 feet per minute at 1500 feet, 2700 f.p.m. at 1000 feet, 2000 f.p.m. at 800 feet and 1600 f.p.m. at 500 feet. In other words, the pilot has less than twenty seconds to avoid a catastrophe.

That twenty seconds has to include reaction time, time to activate the controls, and the seconds needed for a large and ungainly aircraft to reverse its descent and climb out of trouble. Unlike other emergency warnings, for which the standard procedure is to turn off the device, decide what to do and then to act positively, the ground proximity warning system is so critical that the only course of action is to put on power and climb immediately. This is certainly the advice given to its pilots by British Airways, but it is not universal policy among all airlines. Given the dangers, it is quite extraordinary that pilots actually take longer to react to a ground proximity warning than to other emergencies. The read-outs from flight data recorders and cockpit voice-recorders in aircraft involved in incidents shows that pilot response time is a minimum of five seconds. In some cases it has been fifteen seconds or even longer. This compares with an average of between one and four seconds to react to other types of critical warning, depending on the workload in the cockpit at the time.

Why this should be is difficult to tell. Perhaps the warning cry from the device produces such a mental jolt that it actually slows down the pilot's reaction rather than speeding it. Alternatively, it may be that the crew have been conditioned to analyse the situation and verify the warning before acting, or that they believe, deep down, that the system is unreliable. At all events, the situation so worried one speaker at the twenty-ninth international air safety seminar in 1976 that he predicted there would be one accident per year because a pilot did not heed the ground proximity warning until too late. This prediction has proved all too accurate.

The worst disaster thus far in which the ground proximity warning system has figured happened in Antarctica on 28 November 1979 when an Air New Zealand DC10 plunged into the slopes of Mount Erebus. It was an unusual flight – not many wide-bodied airliners are used for sightseeing – and an extraordinary accident. Though Mount Erebus, an active volcano, is 12,000 feet high and the minimum altitude for aircraft in the area is 16,000 feet, the crash actually happened at 1467 feet above sea level.

It all began when Captain Jim Collins spotted a gap in the clouds and decided to give his passengers a closer look at the volcano. Down he went, only to experience a 'white out' as the snow-covered landscape blended with haze and cloud to disorientate the crew. From the cockpit voice-recorder it is clear that they no longer knew where they were. The two flight engineers on board were increasingly worried, but Captain Collins and his first officer took some time to decide that they ought to climb out of danger. They were at 1500 feet before Collins said, 'we'll have to climb out of here,' and he was still discussing with his co-pilot which way they should go when the ground proximity warning sounded. This time there was no twenty seconds of grace: Erebus is a steep mountain. Six and a half seconds later, with full power on, the DC10 ploughed into the icy rock and 257 people, all those on board, were killed instantly.

A Royal Commission report in April 1981 reversed an inquiry finding of pilot error and put the blame on Air New Zealand management for 'faulty operational procedures'. It accused management of 'an orchestrated litany of lies' in its evidence to the inquiry.

The GPWS device is improving all the time and the latest version can give about ten seconds more warning than its predecessor. It was extremely lucky for the captain of a Boeing 747 at Sapporo, Japan, on 1 August, 1979 that his plan was fitted with the new model. An incredible 516 people were on board the Boeing that day, which must be something of a record. They were due to land at Chitose airport but the runway was shrouded in fog and the aircraft was instructed to stand off before being steered in on a radar-controlled approach.

Still the fog was too thick. When only nine miles from the airport and down to 1500 feet, the captain was instructed to turn left on to an easterly heading and to maintain height. Fortunately, as it turned out, he interpreted this to mean his last authorized height, which was 2000 feet, and climbed a little.

Forty-five seconds later the ground proximity device flashed a single warning, but the crew continued on their way. True, the minimum altitude on their charts was 5,400 feet for this area, but presumably they had faith in the ground controllers. After ninety seconds the warning sounded again. This time it was a continuous 'Pull up, pull up!' but for a full fifteen seconds the captain did nothing at all. Then he made a steep climbing turn and diverted the flight to Tokyo. The aircraft had missed the side of a mountain by a scant 500 feet. Had a less advanced warning system been installed, a new and bloody record would have been entered in the annals of civil aviation.

This incident happened fifteen months after the pilot of a National Airlines Boeing 727 had ignored a ground proximity warning and dived into the sea off Florida (see Chapter Four) – and little more than a year after the crash of an Allegheny Airlines BAC111 at Rochester, New York. Communication in the airline industry is none too good.

The Rochester accident was remarkable. One can only suppose that Captain John Johansson was having a bad day, and pray that our own captain is safe from the joint afflictions of blindness and deafness that seemed to overcome this experienced pilot on 9 July, 1978.

Captain Johansson had accumulated 13,461 hours of flying time, 7008 of which he had spent in the BAC111. He was certainly no stranger to the aircraft and presumably knew that its maximum rate of descent on the approach is supposed to be 1000 feet per minute. Nevertheless, as he flew towards the runway at Rochester his altimeter was unwinding at an average of 1240 feet per minute, and, when only 510 feet above the ground, it had reached 2375 feet per minute. His landing speed, which should have been around 118 knots, was in fact 163 knots. What Captain Johansson was doing, having evidently found himself too high on the approach, was 'diving it off' – a common fault among student pilots and a good recipe for disaster. The ground proximity warning worked perfectly in these circumstances: it sounded three times. Captain Johansson took no notice and his first officer did nothing. They could, and should, have aborted the landing and gone round again, but Captain Johansson said later that the idea had not even occurred to him. His aircraft struck the ground nose-first, 2540 feet along the 5,500 foot runway. Even then, at the speed at which it was travelling it could have got back into the air and tried again. What it could not do was stop – which was, of course, what Captain Johansson attempted to do. The 111 shot off the end of the runway, sheering away its under-carriage as it crossed a drainage ditch. At that point the gods of chance relented and put the brakes on Murphy's Law. The next two things which could have gone wrong did not: there was no fire and no solid object stood in the path of the careering airliner. Of the seventy-four passengers and four crew on board, one was seriously injured and nine more slightly hurt.

The event which finally persuaded the FAA to enforce the fitting of ground proximity warning systems in the United States occurred near Washington, DC, on 5 December, 1974. Ironically, or so the subsequent inquiry found, the fate which befell TWA flight 514 that day was due not so much to lack of the proper instruments as the short-comings of the FAA itself – a strange case of safety improvement arising from a cover-up of bureaucratic inefficiency. Still, for whatever reason, it is good to know that almost wherever you fly today the system will be in the cockpit. You may even have a pilot who believes in it and acts upon its warnings.

Flight 514 was a Boeing 727 on a trip from Indianapolis to Washington's National Airport, with a stop along the way at Columbus, Ohio. The pilot, who had returned from a month's leave a week before, was Captain Richard Brock. At forty-four, Brock had spent his entire flying career with TWA, having joined the company in 1955 as a flight engineer and graduated to become a first officer in 1967. He had flown 1557 hours as a captain on the 727. His first officer, Leonard Kresheck, had been with TWA since 1966. Kresheck's total flying time of 2605 hours was also comparatively low for a man of forty. They were joined in the cockpit by the flight engineer, thirty-one-year-old Thomas Safranek.

The four stewardesses who were to cope with the eighty-five passengers on board flight 514 that day were all in their early twenties. Two of them, Denise Stander and Jan Van Fossen, had been hired by TWA less than two months before. They had gone on the training course together, and both had graduated on 7 November. Their careers were destined to be brief, and savagely terminated.

The first stage of the flight, from Indianapolis to Columbus, took an uneventful forty minutes. Prudently, the crew collected an updated weather forecast before setting off again for Washington at 10.24, just eleven minutes behind schedule. The weather was not good: they had been in the air for only twelve minutes when they were informed by Cleveland air-traffic control centre that no landings were being permitted at Washington National because of high crosswinds. The nearest available airport was Dulles, just outside Washington, which is owned and operated by the FAA itself. At 10.42, flight 514 was cleared to divert there.

There was little to be concerned about. Brock and Kresheck calmly discussed the possible routes they might take to Dulles while control was handed routinely from Cleveland to Washington air-traffic control centre and finally to Dulles approach control.

This last hand-over came at 11.01.27, when Brock told the controller that he was descending from 10,000 to 7000 feet. He reported level at the lower altitude at 11.04. 'Flight 514,' replied controller Merle Dameron, 'you are clear for a VOR/DME approach to runway 12.

Unless he is told anything to the contrary, a pilot is entitled to assume that once he receives approach clearance he can descend to the minimum final approach height for that particular airfield and runway. In this case that height was 1800 feet. But flight 514 was still forty-four miles from Dulles, and there were some sizeable hills around.

Captain Brock and his crew had no real reason to doubt

that the controller knew that he was doing. Their diversion had caused them to fly an unpublished route, and it was common practice for controllers to clear aircraft to flyat lower altitudes than those recommended for particular areas. Brock would have known that his controller had information on these possible heights which was not available to him in the cockpit. Like other airline pilots he had become accustomed to this service and, though he did not know exactly where he was in relation to the obstructions on his chart, he trusted the man watching him on the radar screen to see him through.

What Captain Brock did not know was that the radar return to the control centre from his aircraft was obscured by heavy rain and difficult to see. At all events flight 514 started down, bouncing uncomfortably through the turbulent clouds to such an extent that the altimeters were difficult to read. 'Gives you a headache after a while,' commented Kresheck, 'watching this jumping around like that.'

Doubts, vague doubts, were beginning to gather on the flight deck. 'You know,' said Brock at 11.07.35, 'according to this dumb sheet it says 3400 to Round Hill [the VOR navigational beacon] is our minimum altitude.' Round Hill was then 11½ miles away. But then the pilot calmed his own fears. 'When he clears you, that means you can go to your initial approach altitude,' he said.

It was dark inside the cloud and there was still no sign of the ground below them. At 11.08.25 there was a momentary bleep of warning from the radio altimeter.

'I had ground contact a minute ago,' Brock said.

'Yeah, I did too,' Kresheck replied.

The captain warned, 'You've got a high sink rate,' but the flight engineer was unworried.

'We're right there, we're on course,' he said.

Now they were peering anxiously through the murk.

'We ought to see ground outside there in just a minute,' said Brock. 'Hang in there, boy.' Safranek complained that he was getting seasick.

At 11.08.57 the altitude alert sounded again. Kresheck said, 'We must have had a —— of a downdraught.' The warning stopped, only to go off again seventeen seconds later.

By this time Brock was thoroughly alarmed. 'Better get some power on,' he said. They were the last words on the tape of the cockpit voice-recorder. At 11.09.22, in visibility of 50 to 100 feet, flight 514 flew at full tilt into the side of Mount Weather, Virginia. There were no survivors.

Who was to blame? The National Transportation Safety Board, in its subsequent inquiry, found that the FAA had failed to take action to resolve the confusion and misinterpretation caused by air-traffic control terminology, although it had been aware of the problem for 'several years'. It also criticized the fact that an approach clearance had been issued to an aircraft forty-four miles from the runway on an unpublished route and without clearly defined minimum altitudes.

How many more problems are lurking around, known to the authorities but kept from the public, that must wait for an accident to bring them to light? The question is made even more relevant by an extraordinary postscript to the tragedy of flight 514. It seems that some six weeks before the accident an airliner belonging to another company (the identity of which is secret, as usual) had an almost identical experience while approaching the same runway. In this instance the pilot managed to avoid disaster and very properly reported the occurrence to his employers under their anonymous safety-awareness programme. They saw the seriousness of the situation and issued a warning notice to their own flight crews – to their own, but to no one else.

There can be few clearer examples of the appalling and almost criminal lack of communication within certain sectors of the aviation industry. Leaving aside the implications of a safety-awareness programme that has to be anonymous because people are too afraid to risk their own figurative necks to protect the actual lives of others, did the company concerned think that they were the only ones flying into runway 12 at Dulles? Because they failed to pass this information on, and because the FAA had been too dilatory to correct a simple fault of which they had been aware of for years, ninety-two people had to die on a wet and windy Virginia hillside. There is really nothing more to say.

Subsequent to the accident, the FAA shut this particular stable door with a resounding slam. It directed that all commercial airliners be fitted with ground proximity warning systems by December 1975; it revised the provisions for pilot responsibilities and actions after receiving a clearance for a non-precision approach; it changed air-traffic control procedures to provide for the issuance of altitude restrictions during such approaches; and it established an incident-reporting system designed to identify unsafe operating conditions so that they could be corrected before an accident occurred. All very worthy, and just a little late.

Ground proximity warnings notwithstanding, the toll of the mountains goes on. On 4 September, 1977 a Viscount flew into one on its approach to Cuenca, Ecuador, killing the thirty-three passengers and crew on board. The pilot, said the report, had flown the route several times before and was probably over confident.

In July 1979, a Lufthansa Boeing 707 taking off from Rio de Janeiro in rain and fog smashed into a mountainside three minutes after take-off, again with the loss of all lives – though fortunately the flight carried no passengers.

On 14 September, 1979 the pilot of an ATIDC9 near Cagliari, Italy, elected not to follow the published instrument procedure and hit a mountain at 2000 feet, nine miles from the airfield. There were no survivors among the twenty-seven passengers and four crew, nor among those aboard the Boeing 727 of Iran National Airlines which hit a peak while approaching Teheran on 21 January, 1980. 128 people died in this accident, which happened while navigation aids were out of action following a controllers' strike. There have been others . . . many others. Mountain-bashing is an unforgiving pastime, and the only small consolation in this type of accident is that passengers and crew are usually dead before they realize that anything has gone wrong.

At the outset of this chapter I pointed out that mountains were known and predictable hazards. But there is always the exception that proves the rule: witness the salutary experience of British Airways flight BA265 to Panama on the night of 5 October, 1979.

Flight 265 was making its approach on a fine, bright, moonlit night and was cleared by the controller to descend from 5000 to 3600 feet. The pilot queried the instruction because, on his chart, the minimum safety height at that spot was 4100 feet. The controller put his mind at rest. He had him on radar; he was clear to descend. And why not? It was such a clear night that the ground was clearly in sight.

At 3700 feet the ground proximity warning went off. British Airways pilots, you will remember, have strict instructions not to play around when they hear that warning, and this one put on power and climbed away safely. But what could have caused the alarm? There was nothing on the map.

There was, as it turned out, an uncharted peak 3100 feet

high, just eleven miles northeast of Panama airport. A slightly incredulous FAA sent a special aircraft all the way to Panama to have a look. Sure enough, there it was in all its unmapped prominence. 'A very serious discrepancy,' they said in thanking the BA pilot. And well they might. The mountains we know about seem to be quite hazardous enough; myopic cartographers we can all do without.

11
Quit stalling

An aircraft stalls when it is no longer flying fast enough for the wings to generate lift. Actually it gets a bit more complicated than that, but as a general definition this will do well enough. The important thing to remember is that every aeroplane in which you fly has a stalling speed, which is well known to the pilot. Fall below that speed and you begin to drop out of the sky.

Stalling in itself is not particularly dangerous; every student pilot learns how to do it and how to recover from it. It only becomes a hazard if there is insufficient airspace underneath in which to recover from the stall, or from the spin into which it may develop. Nevertheless stalling is not encouraged among airlines, since the practice may lead to loss of passenger confidence, a number of bent aeroplanes and a great wastage of in-flight meals. 'Watch your speed' is a very good piloting dictum, and the man up front is naturally well equipped to do so. Every airliner flying today will have at least two and probably three airspeed indicators.

So there is nothing to worry about, is there? Well, yes and no. The basic airspeed indicator is something that has barely changed since the early days of flying. It consists of a small bellows attached to a pointer, very similar to the common home barometer, and from the cockpit instrument are led two tubes. One goes to a small-diameter probe facing forward into the airstream which is known as the pitot head. The other is connected to a tiny hole on the side of the aircraft and forms the static vent. The difference between the pressure in the two tubes acts upon the bellows to tell the pilot how fast he is travelling through the air. At least, it gives him his indicated airspeed. Since the density and temperature of the air vary according to altitude, his true airspeed is somewhat different and his groundspeed – affected by the wind – is something else again. But let's not get too technical. For the purpose of falling, or not falling, out of the sky, indicated airspeed (IAS) is what matters.

It is not a bad system. Without gyros or complex electronics there is precious little to go wrong – but there is one snag. The ends of those two tubes, on which the airspeed indicator depends totally for its function, are exposed to the elements during every moment of flight. They face winds near the speed of sound at temperatures many degrees below zero. They pass through rain and hail and snow and fog. Most important of all, they are exposed to icing conditions. For any aircraft, ice is a major hazard. Its build-up on wings and tail surfaces can have a catastrophic effect, not only through increased weight but because, by altering the aerofoil shape, ice can seriously affect their lifting capacity. Not to worry: modern aircraft are always sprayed with anti-freeze before they take off in arctic conditions and all have efficient de-icing systems to take care of things once they are airborne. The vital pitot head that carries the rushing wind to the airspeed indicator has its own built-in heating element. But the static vent usually does not. There would be nothing very difficult about heating this minute opening in the aircraft's skin and in terms of expense, the sum involved would be derisory compared with the total cost of the machine. Yet tradition has it that heating is unnecessary because the static vent is always placed in a position where, according to aeronautical engineers, icing will not take place. The only trouble with this theory is that engineers sometimes get it wrong.

On 7 December, 1978, a British Airways Trident III was making a routine flight from Belfast to London Heathrow in the early evening. The Trident, flight 4663, was flying at 13,000 feet and butting its way into a 40-knot wind blowing from 170 degrees. It was raining heavily, cloud cover was total and the temperature outside the aircraft ranged from minus 2 to minus 4 degrees Centigrade. It was a typically nasty English December night and the icing conditions were rated as moderate to severe.

When it reached Bovingdon to the west of London, flight 4663 was instructed to hold its position until it could be fitted into the stream of traffic waiting to land. The first officer was in control with the autopilot engaged, and he reduced the indicated airspeed to 210 knots with the leading-edge slats extended. Two of the three engines were connected to the auto-throttle, while the third was left at 11,200 r.p.m. to cope with the needs of cabin pressurization and the airframe anti-icing system. Though the cloud was not thick and there was no turbulence, the cockpit was lit up by the eerie effect of St Elmo's fire on the windscreens. There was much static on the radio.

The Trident continued its steady circle in the holding pattern. At one point an ice warning sounded, but the flight engineer reported that all seemed to be well and it was switched off. Just to be on the safe side, the captain checked that his pitot-head heaters were switched on and working; they were.

It was during their last outbound turn, when they were slowly descending, that an odd discrepancy showed up. Though the airspeed indicators were still registering 210 knots, the Doppler device which measures speed over the ground had dropped to 135 knots. Had they suddenly run into a very strong headwind? The first officer commented that their rate of descent, at around 400 feet per minute, was very low.

Something odd was going on. Again, the pilot checked the pitot-head heaters, but all was normal and the previous ice warning had cleared. He called for a cross-check of the aircraft's attitude and the first officer reported that his artificial horizon showed that they were flying about 8 degrees nose-up. At that moment the Trident stalled. The control columns shook violently as the automatic warning system came into operation and flight 4663 began to sag out of the sky.

There was no time for delay. Reacting instinctively, the captain took over the controls, disengaged the autopilot and levelled the wings to prevent a relatively harmless stall from developing into a vicious spin. He lowered the nose by pushing forward on the control column and called for more power. The airspeed indicator moved rapidly to 250 knots – well above stalling speed – and the captain raised the nose again to contain the acceleration and called for the leading-edge slats to be raised. Nothing happened. The baulk device which prevents the slats on a Trident being retracted at too low a speed (product of a previous nasty accident) was still in operation. Yet by this time the pilot's airspeed indicator had reached 280 knots and the first officer's back-up instrument carried the same reading. Something, somewhere, was awfully wrong. By implication, both instruments were overreading, but the amount of error was anybody's guess.

Old-time pilots could tell how fast they were travelling by the sound of the wind in the wires and the feel of its blast on their face. Their modern counterpart has no such aid. Without an airspeed indicator which he can trust he is like a blind man walking on the edge of a cliff. At 11,000 feet there was no great problem – but how were the crew of flight 4663 to judge their critical speed on the approach to land? A stall at this stage of the flight would mean certain death for all on board.

The first officer re-applied power as the captain attempted to regain level flight, but there was another minor stall. At this stage the aircraft was heading westwards and a tart reminder came from the ground controller, watching the odd progress of flight 4663 on radar, that they were not cleared to leave the holding pattern. He was rapidly told of the instrument failure, and granted a priority approach to Heathrow. Then, as suddenly as it had begun, the emergency ended. The airspeed indicators fluttered in unison and fell back to 180 knots. This checked out with the stand-by airspeed indicator, located on the Trident III in a position where it cannot easily be seen by either pilot. This time the instruments had got it right and the Trident landed safely.

What had happened was that the static vent had been blocked by ice, leaving the airspeed indicators with no counter-force to the pressure from the pitot head. The autopilot, getting its information from the same source, had quietly pushed the nose up to check the apparent speed to the point where the aircraft stalled. Long investigation by the Civil Aviation Authority in conjunction with British Aerospace came up with the innovative idea that it might be a good idea to heat the static vents on the Trident.

This has now been done. Why, you may ask, was it not thought of when the aircraft was first designed? Indeed, why is it not done on all aircraft as a matter of course? The answer would probably be that this particular fault has not yet killed anyone. Yet a similar problem can affect the ordinary altimeter (as opposed to the new radio altimeters) which also depends on a static vent for accurate reading. And ice blockage of *that* vent has certainly killed people: to be precise, the fifty passengers and crew of a TWA jet which crashed a mile short of its destination on 20 November, 1967.

Of course, even when safeguards are provided they are not always used. Take the case of the Boeing 727 of North West Airlines which took off from J.F. Kennedy airport, New York, on 1 December, 1974. The story of flight 6231 is briefly told: it lasted only twelve minutes, by which time it had climbed to 24,800 feet. At this point it stalled and began to spin until, at 3500 feet, part of the tailplane broke off. From this moment the fatal crash was inevitable. The cause was later found to be the crew's failure to turn on the pitot-head heaters, which caused them to get a false reading from the airspeed indicators. The pilot apparently never realized what was happening and the mistake cost the lives of himself, his first officer and the flight engineer. By lucky chance this was a ferry flight and there were no passengers on board.

There were passengers, however, on the Vickers Viscount of the Swedish airline Linjeflyg which crashed near Stockholm on 15 January, 1977. The Viscount was making its final approach to Bromma airfield, and was about three miles from the end of the runway at 1150 feet, when it suddenly went into a vertical dive from which there was no hope of recovery. Nor was there any hope of survival for the nineteen passengers and three crew.

The cause was ice on the tailplane which had caused the airflow to break away and thus induce a stall. It had accumulated because two of the engines had been on low power for a long time, thus lessening the efficiency of the anti-icing system. It was another accident which need never have happened. The Viscount has been around for a long time, and its slight predilection for tailplane icing was well known. Yet there were incomplete instructions in the official flight manual and too little information in the company's own operations manual concerning the consequences of such icing. Poor communication had claimed another twenty-two victims. How many more will there be this year?

More fortunate were the fifty passengers on an Aerolinias Argentinas Boeing 707 which took off from New York on 14 January, 1977 with snow and ice on the wings and in the middle of a snowstorm. The pilot had only just taken off when a static-ridden radio message was heard in the control tower. 'We are in a stall . . . just recovered from a stall at 200 feet.' Though 200 feet is about as close to a stall disaster as one can get without actually scraping the wreckage off the ground, the pilot refused to return for an emergency landing but continued on his merry way. He had, he said, got the aircraft under control.

One of the passengers gave a less laconic account of what had happened. He claimed that the plane shuddered – the usual symptom at the onset of a stall – and dived towards the ground three times, just missing the houses below. An engine spewed flames, stewardesses burst into tears and his fellow passengers were in a state of panic. He later complained to the authorities, and it is hard to blame him. Perhaps more people should – if only they knew what was going on up there.

12

Into the vortex

If ice and snow, rain and wind, fog and thunderstorms are dangerous for flying, at least one should be fairly safe on calm and sunny summer afternoons. What a pleasure to fly on such a day. There you are, snug in the seat of your medium-haul jet, seatbelt fastened as the overhead light goes on and the pilot begins his long smooth descent to your holiday airport. The patchwork fields below you begin to come alive; you can almost feel the heat reflecting off the red-tiled roofs, smell the cooking and taste the wine. Off to your right, the blue mirror of the sea is specked with slack-sailed yachts, and your toes wiggle in anticipation of white sand.

Then, all of a sudden, you are upside down. Your drink, 500 magazines and a stewardess or two are bouncing off the roof. The cabin is filled with screams and chaos as the pilot crams on power and fights a desperate battle to get the aircraft upright and save you all from plunging to the ground.

What happened? What could possibly have happened on such a lovely day in a brand-new aircraft, manned by a crew who have impressed you with their competence and skill all the way?

Can you see that Boeing 747 in front of us? No, of course you can't see it from your window. As a matter of fact, the pilot could hardly see it either because it was four miles in front of us before it landed and taxied off the runway. But that jumbo was responsible for what just happened to you.

Not intentionally, for he was flying perfectly properly. But every aircraft trails behind it a tornado, or rather two tornadoes. They are known as wing-tip vortices and the larger the aircraft and the more slowly it is flying, the more powerful they become. In the case of that 747, those spiral vortices were probably travelling at 100 miles per hour. They sink slowly downwards and roll away from one another, but when the day is warm and the wind is calm as it is today they hang around for a long time. You cannot see them, there is nothing to tell the following pilot that they are there, but once his wing flies into the vortex it is as though a giant hand has picked it up or thrust it down.

Complete inversion in this sort of situation is fortunately rare, though it has happened. More frequent is an uncontrollable bank through 45 or even 90 degrees and when this happens at very low altitude, as it usually does, the danger is very great. On 26 September, 1978, a small Beechcraft and an Eastern Airlines 747 were on final approach together for the runway at San Juan, Puerto Rico. The 747, with a much faster approach speed, overtook the twin-engined Beechcraft to land first, passing overhead at a distance of about 500 feet. This in itself is hardly a recommended manoeuvre. In this case, because of the wing-tip vortices, the result was fatal. The Beechcraft went out of control and crashed two and a half miles short of the runway, killing all six people on board plus two in a car on the ground.

Nor are the effects of these cyclones limited to small aircraft, though these are far more vulnerable. On 2 June, 1977, a British Airways jumbo taking off from New York for a flight to London had reached 1000 feet before it rolled rapidly to the right. The airspeed, which had been a comfortable 171 knots, fell off to a dangerous 155 knots and brought the 747 very close to a stall from which it might not have recovered in the height available. Luckily, with prompt recovery action by the pilot, the aircraft was stabilized safely. But not before all concerned had gone through a very anxious fifteen seconds.

The cause of this incident was the vortex wake from an Air France 747 which had taken off ninety seconds before. Acccording to air-traffic control at Kennedy airport, the British pilot was warned of the danger.

The captain of a Boeing 727 attempting to land at Seattle was equally lucky. Just short of the runway, only 200 feet above the ground, he lost complete control of the aircraft as it ran into the wake left by a 747 which had been five miles in front of him. The jumbo had been too high on the approach and had decided to abort its landing and go round again – which may well have left its wing-tip vortices hanging high in the almost calm conditions that day. The 727 pilot reported that the air was perfectly smooth until he reached 200 feet, at which point he met a violent down-draught. 'The aeroplane quit flying,' he said laconically later. He was down to 50 feet before control was re-established, no more than a hiccup from disaster.

Recognition of the vortex problem has led to recommendations for the air-traffic control spacing of jet aircraft. UK standards are set higher than those for the rest of the world; for a medium-sized aircraft following a heavy wide-body, for instance, the ICAO standard is a separation of five miles or two minutes of flying time. In Britain the standard is six miles and three minutes.

These standards, plus an increasing awareness of the danger, have undoubtedly improved the situation. The number of British aircraft involved in vortex wake incidents has fallen from twenty-five in 1976 to ten in 1977, seven in 1978 and only three in the first half of 1979. Nevertheless, as with mid-air collisions, the risk persists at busy airports where controllers cannot cope with the volume of traffic without bending the regulations.

Almost as difficult to spot as wing-tip vortices, and completely immune to man-made rules and controls, are birds. To airmen they are a constant hazard. The measures to keep them away from airports, where they present the greatest danger, are many and various. Distress calls, random explosions, hawks and kites, and even systematic shooting have all been tried. These methods have one thing in common: none of them work completely. Birds are regularly sucked into the intakes of jet engines where they tend to prove indigestible.

The problem is getting worse rather than better. In 1976 and 1977 only seventeen British aircraft suffered from bird-strikes. In 1978 the total went up to twenty-six and there were eighteen in the first six months of 1979 alone – the last period for which figures are available.

The most dangerous airports are those near the coast, which tend to attract large flocks of seabirds. One major seaboard terminal in the United States recently had twenty-seven bird-strike accidents in a single year; for American airlines, the annual cost of engine repairs alone necessitated by bird-strikes is running at more than $4 million.

The total cost, of course, is far greater – not to mention the risk to human life. On 21 November, 1975, a DC 10 of Overseas International Airlines – value around $50 million – was completely destroyed by fire after one of its engines ingested a large number of seagulls at New York's J.F. Kennedy airport. The Port Authority of New York and New Jersey used shotgun patrols to control the bird population at Kennedy and had stepped up its efforts less than two weeks before the crash. This accident showed the ineffectiveness of such action . . . and revealed a few other shortcomings in addition.

As the DC 10 sped down the runway, carrying 139 airline employees on a trans-Atlantic ferry flight, it struck a large flock of seagulls at a speed of 100 knots. Twenty dead birds were later found on the runway, the biggest of which weighed 5 pounds. The effect on the aircraft was catastrophic. One engine disintegrated and caught fire, causing the loss of an hydraulic system which in turn halved the braking efficiency of the DC10. Its capacity to stop was further impaired by the loss of reverse thrust on the failed engine and the fact that two of the ten spoilers refused to extend. To make matters worse, at least three of the tyres disintegrated . . . and the runway was wet.

It was shrapnel from the engine which punctured the tyres, fuel tanks and hydraulic system; the engine had blown up because damage caused by the birds had unbalanced the turbine. And therein lies another tale.

The DC10 was fitted with General Electric CF6 engines which had drilled-tip compressor blades. This was a new-technology development aimed at improving engine performance and was certified by the FAA under a 'special conditions' procedure which allows manufacturers to set their own certification standards if they can provide a satisfactory engineering basis for an exception to the existing standards. Although it was later learned that General Electric had based its application on standards devised for a rival Pratt and Whitney engine, and that the FAA was well aware that drilled-tip blades could not withstand bird-strikes, nothing was done. The FAA refused to issue an order compelling replacement of the blades with the well-proven solid variety. Nor, in spite of the known hazard, had the manufacturer ever taken into account the effect of an unbalanced turbine during its tests. The FAA had not required GE to do so.

It seems pertinent to ask, Why not? After all, birds have been around for a few million years, and have been bumping into aeroplanes since the days of the Wright brothers. A congressional sub-committee set up after this accident found the answer. Its report concluded, 'When the engine and later the aircraft encountered certification difficulties, the respective manufacturers of each descended on the FAA to forestall further testing and to expedite the certification process. This can no doubt be expected, but the FAA must resist any such pressures to shortcut its procedures. There can be no accommodations when considerations of safety must be paramount.'

The wider implications of this revelation by the congressmen are quite chilling. So far as this particular problem is concerned, is it beyond the power of human ingenuity to think up a device which will keep birds out of jet engines? Surely not.

In the Kennedy incident it was a minor miracle that the pilot managed to steer his crippled machine onto a taxiway and evacuate the passengers without fatal injury (although thirty-two people were hurt, two of them seriously). If they had not, by pure chance, all been airline employees well schooled in emergency procedures, the story might have been different.

Nor is the problem confined to jet engines and large birds. On 25 July 1978, with the clouds lowering down to only 100 feet above the runway, a Convair 580 twin-engined turbo-prop took off from Kalamazoo in the United States. The bird that flew into the left-hand engine air intake weighted no more than four ounces. None the less, it was sufficient to cause a transient compressor stall in the engine. By itself this was nothing to worry about but, as is so often the case in aviation mishaps, one thing led to another.

The Convair 580 is fitted with an auto-feathering device intended to increase safety by cutting the drag from the propeller should an engine fail. Unfortunately it is so sensitive that even a momentary interruption of power such as happened on this occasion will set it off and deprive the pilot of half his engines at a critical moment in flight. The pilot's handbook for the aircraft is aware of this problem and actually suggests, 'During take-off, if birds are observed adjacent to or in the path of the take-off pattern, disarm the auto-feather circuit.' But Kalamazoo does not, officially, have a bird problem. The Catch 22 is that if a pilot takes the handbook advice, deactivates the auto-feather for fear of birds and then loses an engine for some other reason, he may crash anyway because of the increased drag on the powerless wing. As one safety expert commented after the Kalamazoo incident, 'Considering the shallowness of our accident sense, this twenty-year-old problem will not be resolved until a pilot rolls his aircraft into a ball, following a true engine failure on take-off with the auto-feather system deactivated because of a bird hazard.'

The pilot of the Kalamazoo Convair was torn between two courses of action: either he could return to the runway and make an emergency landing – a hazardous operation with low cloud and visibility down to half a mile – or he could carry on with the flight. The latter choice carried the danger that he would lose his one remaining engine.

In the event he did neither. In the confusion of the moment he had forgotten to raise the undercarriage and, as the aircraft entered the cloud eight seconds after take-off, the drag from the wheels plus a turn towards the feathered engine made further flight impossible. He managed to avoid some obstacles as he came out of the cloud and made a successful crash-landing in a cornfield. His shaken passengers survived, unlike the sixty-two who died in an almost identical accident in 1960.

If we are to fly with the birds we will have to live with them. Just pray that they keep well clear of your particular aeroplane.

13
Unlucky for some

The DC10 which crashed at Chicago on 25 May 1979 did more than snuff out the lives of 273 people: it also opened a can of worms in the overtly spotless kitchen of aviation safety. There was more at stake than the reputation of a singularly unlucky airliner. The investigations which followed disclosed a malaise which must bring grave concern to each and every one of us who fly. Regrettably, much of this material has never been made known to the general public. Though the inquiries were diligent and ranged much wider than this particular crash, their results were expressed in jargon difficult to read and even harder to comprehend. It is only when you cut through the gobbledygook, ignore the split infinitives and get down to the meat of the matter that the true horror of the picture emerges. In this chapter and that which follows, I will try to do just that.

The story of the disaster itself is well known. At the point of lift-off, the left-hand engine of flight 191, a DC10 belonging to American Airlines, fell off. To be more precise, it came adrift at the pylon attachment point on the wing and rotated forwards and upwards under its own immense thrust until it went right over the wing and fell to the ground. Hydraulic and electrical systems were torn out in the process.

On the flight deck, from which it is impossible to see the engines, Captain Walter Lux knew only that he had lost power on the left-hand side. He tried to do what the

American Airlines flight manual told him to do in the event of a failed engine on take-off: to maintain V2 (153 knots), which is the minimum climbing speed for a DC10 with two engines working and the leading-edge slats extended. Since his speed of 173 knots was well in excess of V2, he decided to trade speed for height and allowed his speed to drop to 153 knots as he climbed away – no doubt intending to circle the field and make an emergency landing. This was strictly according to the book.

Captain Lux had no way of knowing that two vital cockpit warning systems had been disabled by the separation of the engine. One of these was the slat disagreement device, which should have told him that the six outboard leading-edge slats on the left wing had retracted. The effect of this retraction was to increase the stalling speed on the left wing to 159 knots, and it was a classic case of Murphy's Law that the other warning system to be destroyed was the stick-shaker which gives the pilot advance notice of a stall.

So when Captain Lux tried to climb away on his remaining two engines – a feat of which the DC10 was perfectly capable – he unwittingly allowed the left wing to stall. From this point there was nothing that could be done to avert disaster. Deprived of half its lift, the stricken DC10 fell on to its left side and dived into the ground. The worst domestic air crash in US aviation history had run its course.

The subsequent investigation was of furious intensity. The FAA, which at one point lost its head and grounded the worldwide fleet of DC10s for reasons which later proved unjustified, eventually produced a report more than 5000 pages long. The NTSB produced another and it was ultimately agreed that the engine had fallen off because of 'improper maintenance procedures' by American Airlines. What the airline's engineers had been doing, as the world now knows, was to use a fork-lift truck to remove engine and pylon together for maintenance, replacing them in the same way. By acting thus instead of using the standard procedure of taking the engine from the pylon first, they were saving 200 man hours per aircraft and a considerable amount of money. Unfortunately, they had also cracked the airframe and killed a lot of people.

But there was much more to it than that. It emerged that American Airlines, which was later fined half a million dollars for its sins by the FAA, had actually consulted McDonnell Douglas, designer and builder of the DC10, before starting to use the fork-lift truck procedure. McDonnell Douglas, it is true, had not encouraged the operation; but neither had the company given it their explicit disapproval. American Airlines decided that was good enough, and went ahead and did it. After all, it would save money – or so management thought. Nor was American Airlines the only operator to adopt this procedure. Continental Airlines was also using fork-lift trucks to remove engine/pylon assemblies on the DC10. But Continental (and its passengers) were lucky. Two pylon flanges were broken but they were spotted and repaired before they could cause a disaster.

This happened before the Chicago crash. It was a classic case of one operator gaining information which could be of benefit to the safety of the whole industry but, as usual, the news was never passed on. Continental did, in fact, report the failures to McDonnell Douglas. For reasons best known to themselves, McDonnell Douglas notified its customers of the first instance of the later fatal maintenance damage in a low-priority Operational Occurrences Report of which American Airlines had no memory and which Continental discovered in its service library after the accident. Once again a failure to communicate had proved fatal.

For its part in the sorry story, Continental Airlines was fined $100,000 by the FAA. McDonnell Douglas, whose aircraft was ultimately declared safe and allowed back into the air, did not escape unscathed either. Aside from the enormous psychological damage to the reputation of the DC10, which damaged sales and led to a glut of the aircraft on the secondhand market, the manufacturer was criticized for not considering at the design stage the vulnerability of the structure to damage during maintenance. In several places, said the NTSB report, clearances were unnecessarily small, making maintenance difficult to perform and encouraging the sort of short cut which led to disaster. This was not only an attack on McDonnell Douglas but also on the FAA, which had certified the design in the first place. Even more worrying, from a passenger's point of view, was the fact that McDonnell Douglas was fined $300,000 for 'quality control deficiencies' not related to the Chicago crash.

Why should this worry us? The Federal Aviation Authority, which imposed this fine, is responsible for the safe design, manufacture and maintenance of every aircraft made in the United States. More civil aircraft are built in that country than anywhere else in the world: we all fly in them. Yet here was the FAA, inspired by a single crash, suddenly making investigations which disclosed that one of the manufacturers under its wing had been turning out aeroplanes with a design fault. This was not so much a reflection on McDonnell Douglas as a damning indictment of the FAA itself, which had clearly been failing to do the job it was set up to do. How closely has it supervised other manufacturers over the years, and how well is it doing its job today? Whatever the answers to those questions, it is certain beyond peradventure that many of us are flying in aircraft made before the events of 25 May

1979 concentrated the bureaucratic mind.

Before returning to this point and explaining just how the FAA came to be caught with its trousers round its ankles, there is one outstanding aspect of the Chicago crash which must be dealt with. Talk to experienced flyers about the accident today and you will still hear that it could have been avoided by the pilot. If only, they say, Captain Lux had lowered the nose and gained airspeed instead of striving for height, the disaster would never have happened. This is true up to a point, though it is a fair bet that few of the critics would wish to have been in the left-hand seat of that DC10 on the day in question. Theorizing is one thing; split-second action is another.

And the charge misses the point that not only was Captain Lux doing what he had been trained to do in such a situation, but he was denied the only warning devices which would have persuaded him to do otherwise. In fact he flew the aircraft successfully for thirty seconds after the engine fell off, before the fatal stall occurred at a speed which the flight manual said was safe!

Once all this had been realized, and it was common knowledge before the DC10 was allowed back into the air on 13 July 1979, it may have seemed prudent to amend the flight manual to save any future pilots from being caught in the same trap as Captain Lux and his passengers. Not a bit of it. Though American Airlines did change the recommendations in its own handbook to allow its DC10 pilots an extra 10 knots of airspeed to play with, the FAA refused to issue a general recommendation. Having been told by the manufacturer that the dual malfunction of an engine and the leading-edge slats was 'extremely improbable' – irrespective of the fact that it had happened – the authority issued a statement on 6 August saying: 'We have considered the need for raising the V2 speeds to further reduce (*sic*) this danger and have concluded that the small benefit obtained is insufficient to outweigh its adverse impact.' One FAA official, Mr Charles Foster, even went so far as to describe the suggestion that the V2 speed instructions be raised as 'foolish'. He should have tried telling that to Captain Lux and 272 others.

Then, four months later on 28 November, the FAA performed a complete volte-face and approved a change in the DC10 flight manual for all operators, on the lines already implemented by American Airlines. There was no explanation – but whenever did you hear a civil servant admit he has made a mistake?

Anyway, the minor embarrassment of this incident was as nothing compared with what was to come. It was the misfortune of the FAA to be under investigation by a Congressional committee at the time of the DC10 crash. Led by Representative Jack Brooks from Texas, the thirty-eight Congressmen had already spent several months inquiring into the authority's activities when the accident happened and it is clear from reading their report that it stirred them into a frenzy of activity.

Published on 7 May 1980, the sixteenth report by the Committee on Government Operations, entitled *A Thorough Critique of Certification of Transport Category Aircraft by the Federal Aviation Administration*, does not sound like ideal bedside reading. Nor is it, unless you are prepared to be frightened away from flying ever, ever again.

Let us start with the DC10 and those mysterious quality-control deficiencies which cost McDonnell Douglas $300,000. This horror story goes back to 1974, when the engine pylon assembly line was moved from Douglas's Santa Monica factory to its Huntington Beach facility. Many skilled workers declined to move with the assembly line. Then in the summer of 1978, the work was moved again within the Huntington factory. All the time, demand for the DC10 was burgeoning and, as the delivery schedule increased, there was a decline in the level of skilled labour and spare parts.

Still, everything seemed to be all right. Between 17 July and 25 August 1978, the FAA actually conducted one of its rare 'quality assurance system analysis review' audits at several Douglas plants including that at Huntington Beach. It found nothing wrong – at least with the building of the pylons. It was not until after the Chicago crash, when every DC10 ever built came under microscope, that it was discovered that between twenty-five and thirty DC10s had been delivered with defective pylon assemblies between 1974 and 1979. Some of these had actually been constructed while the FAA audit was in progress. One pylon on a United Airlines DC10 was so defective that the loose engine could be shaken by hand. The others had between two and twenty-six faulty fasteners in each assembly. By the time they were discovered, some were ready to 'unzip', that is break down, under normal operating stress. By some miracle, none had caused an accident. Yet had it not been for Chicago it seems unlikely that they would have been found in time.

This was one fault on one manufacturer's aircraft that happened to have a large enough crash to cause a major uproar. How many more aircraft are waiting to surprise us all by falling apart one day?

Though the airworthiness authorities of other countries, including the British CAA, can and do impose their own standards on American aircraft, the major responsibility still lies with the FAA. It is this body which approves the original design criteria and if things go wrong at this stage there is not much that can be done later. The same is true of faults in manufacture and maintenance. Though FAA supervision only affects US carriers, those airlines are themselves operating world-wide and selling tickets to passengers of all nationalities. Thus the shortcomings of the FAA, if they exist, ought to concern us all.

There was certainly no doubt in the minds of the Congressional Committee on Government Operations that something was very wrong with the FAA. Nor were its members the first to launch such an attack. Even in the United States, where public agencies are scrutinized to a degree which would make the British civil service blanch with horror if it ever suffered such inquiry, the FAA must hold the record for having its dirty linen washed in open view. Not that it seems to have had much effect.

The root of the problem lies with the fact that the FAA has a dual statutory mandate. It is charged with promoting air commerce and, at the same time, ensuring 'the highest practicable level of safety'. This is like asking God and Mammon to work in the same office. The winner of the incessant conflict between safety and profit is all too predictable. Not that any manufacturer, in the US or elsewhere, ever deliberately made an unsafe aircraft. Nor did any airline set out to make one crash. But under the stress of commercial pressure short cuts are taken and the letter of the law sometimes ignored.

As the Brooks Committee pointed out:

There are subtle countervailing forces which make it difficult for those in the industry who are paid to worry about equipment failures and safety to do so and to make their voices heard by decision makers. Precise delivery dates and schedules must be met by competing manufacturers, even if design or maintenance problems are insufficiently resolved. And airlines operating increasingly expensive aircraft must maximize revenues. A complex arrangement of large investments in aircraft and equipment between manufacturer and airlines generates enormous economic pressure to minimize FAA intervention, particularly when delays or changes in certification procedures or standards result, or when expensive modifications or more required inspections must be made.

It is precisely because of this 'enormous economic pressure' that the passenger needs a strong policemen to protect his interests. The FAA looks all too often like a bent copper. The committee put it more diplomatically, but the message is clear:

Over the years, the FAA has become dangerously oriented to the needs of industry management at the expense of the travelling public. FAA's inspectors often seem to act as management consultants rather than informed regulators with a variety of investigating and disciplinary tools at their disposal, and a mandate to use them. Despite the protestation of the current FAA Administrator to the contrary, evidence indicates many FAA personnel and policies seem oriented towards promoting or protecting the industry's economic well-being rather than maintaining the highest possible level of safety.

There is wide agreement that the FAA is understaffed and severely lacking in the expertise needed if it is to make valid judgements on highly sophisticated modern aircrcraft technology. Its inspectors are not paid sufficiently well and nor do they have the sort of career structure needed to attract men of the highest calibre. That is why the FAA relies to a great extent on designated engineering representatives, known as DERs, to do its work. And therein lies the rub. The DERs, who check each stage of an aircraft's design on behalf of the FAA, are paid by the manufacturers. They are no doubt skilled and competent engineers, but where does their main loyalty lie?

On the maintenance side of the industry, the committee found 'major deficiencies':

Needed maintenance has been consistently deferred, quality control departments are made ineffective in any number of ways, and airline inspectors and mechanics may be poorly trained.

Most important, the FAA's system of defect reporting and analysis has become so outdated and ineffective that the agency all too frequently is unable to detect important defects in design,

manufacture or maintenance. As the FAA Administrator himself has indicated, the FAA might have prevented the Chicago
accident had this deficiency been corrected.

The Administrator at the time, Mr Langhorne Bond – a
political appointee of the Carter regime – had told the
committee in evidence:

We found that no pattern appeared in our computers that would
have alerted us to special problems in the engine/pylon area. No
such pattern emerged because the proper information had not
been fed into the computers. And it wasn't fed into the computers because our regulations didn't require that it be reported
to us. I am moving to correct that situation.

Not before time, one might think, and the committee
viewed Mr Bond's conversion to the cause of safety with a
certain cynical reserve. They remembered, and took some
satisfaction in pointing out, that this was the man who told
the National Aviation club in Washington that he wasn't
worried about the machinery used in aviation – that the
whole sophisticated system was incredibly reliable.

The date of this confident statement by Mr Bond was 16
March 1979 – only ten weeks before the Chicago crash –
and the committee had some reason for believing that the
Administrator would be no more in favour of reforming
the certification process after the disaster than he was
before it. After all, nothing much had happened after the
promises to tighten up safety which followed the previous
DC10 tragedy in 1974.

In some ways, the crash of the Turkish Airlines DC10
outside Paris on 3 March 1974 was an even worse indictment of the FAA than what happened in Chicago. The
airliner had stopped in the French capital on its way from
Istanbul to London; its take-off had then been delayed by
the late arrival of a large number of passengers. When it
finally roared down the runway and lifted into the air, it
was carrying 334 passengers and a crew of eleven. All went

well for eight minutes, until the DC10 reached a height of 12,000 feet. Then the controllers on the ground heard an exclamation from the pilot in Turkish, a lot of background noise and cockpit warnings that the pressurization had failed and the aircraft was going too fast. Then there was nothing. The radar blip broke in two and the secondary radar label disappeared from the screen. Seventy seconds later, watchers on the ground saw the airliner coming down in a shallow high-speed dive, striking treetops and finally disintegrating in the forest at Ermonville, just outside Paris. There were no survivors.

The cause of the disaster was the aft cargo door on the left-hand side which had fallen off because it was not properly fastened. The sudden decompression caused the floor of the DC10 to collapse, taking with it six passengers and destroying the flying controls to the tail surfaces. Without these it was impossible for the pilot to regain control. All on board were condemned from that instant.

There can have been few instances of more useless or more culpable deaths in the air, for the problem with DC10 cargo doors was well known in March 1974. It was known to the manufacturers, it was known to the airlines and it was known to the FAA. Only the passengers were left in blind ignorance. The danger had been spotted more than three years before by an engineer working for a sub-contractor to McDonnell Douglas. He predicted that the door-latch mechanism could fail, and with it the floor of the passenger cabin. His report was ignored and the FAA was not informed. During a static test on an assembled fuselage, the engineer's theory was proved correct; but still no design changes were made. The DC10s certificate of airworthiness was granted on 29 July 1971 and the airliner entered service without restrictions or reservations. According to the FAA and the firm who built it, the DC10 was safe.

During the ensuing months, McDonnell Douglas received more than 100 complaints about the cargo door from four of its customer airlines. Not one was passed on to the FAA. Then, on 12 June 1972, something happened near Windsor, Ontario.

A DC10 of American Airlines was climbing out of nearby Detroit that day when, at an altitude of 11,750 feet, the cargo door fell off. In accordance with the prediction, the passenger floor collapsed, but luckily the flight was only carrying a light load of fifty-six passengers and eleven crew and none of them was sucked out. Even more fortunately, in spite of damage to the control cables the pilot was able to get command of the aircraft again and make an emergency landing. Two stewardesses and nine passengers suffered minor injuries; the rest just got an awful fright. After that, the problem could no longer be ignored. Nor was it. The FAA could have issued an Airworthiness Directive, compelling the manufacturer to redesign the door latch and strengthen the passenger flooring on all DC10s then flying or under construction. What the authority did, in fact, was to make a polite telephone call to McDonnell Douglas, who then issued a service bulletin which simply recommended that action be taken but did not require it.

Bearing in mind the history of the problem – original warning, the complaints by airlines and the Windsor incident – such action by the FAA showed a Panglossian faith in the aviation industry that was naïve to say the least. At least one DC10 still at its plant awaiting delivery to a customer was not modified. The customer was Turkish Airlines. The aircraft was the one which crashed in Paris.

On 9 July 1974, the FAA sprang into action and prosecuted McDonnell Douglas for failing to make the modification on two DC10s, including the one which had crashed. The total fine was $2000 – hardly a powerful deterrent to a large corporation.

The latch on the cargo door was a small thing, but deadly. So was the little matter of the cockpit control handles for the ground spoilers on another McDonnell Douglas aircraft, the DC8. Ground spoilers are one of the devices deployed after landing to kill the lift on the wings and help bring the aircraft to rest. The trouble with the DC8 was that a small movement in the wrong direction could deploy the spoilers in flight. Not a good idea.

It happened on 5 July 1970, when a DC8 operated by Air Canada was approaching to land at Toronto with 100 passengers and nine crew on board. Everything seemed to be going well until the four-engined jet was about 60 feet from the ground; then it seemed to drop from the sky. The pilot attempted to recover but struck the runway so hard that number four engine fell off. The DC8 bounced into the air and climbed straight ahead until it reached 3000 feet. There were several explosions; number three engine fell off together with a large part of the right wing. The aircraft fell to the ground, killing all on board.

When the flight data recorder was recovered from the wreckage it showed that 'for some undetermined reason' the ground spoilers had been prematurely deployed.

This time the FAA did issue an Airworthiness Directive, but all this said was that pilots should not deploy ground spoilers in flight. A Congressional sub-committee later described this as 'almost totally worthless' and roughly equivalent to 'warning pilots not to crash their aircraft'.

Nothing was done about the design of the control handles. Not, that is, until 1973, when McDonnell Douglas was finally persuaded by its customers (not by the FAA) to make a design modification. By then a further sixty-one people had died when a Japanese Air Lines DC8 extended its spoilers and crashed just after taking off from Moscow.

As Captain J. J. O'Donnell, president of the Air Line Pilots Association, commented later, 'It was clearly a cockpit design deficiency that could have and should have been caught before the first aircraft ever took to the air. Typically, no one in authority paid any attention until a number of lives were lost.'

It may seem that this chapter has been hard on McDonnell Douglas, and on the DC10 in particular. Well, facts are facts. But perhaps it is only fair to give some on the other side. In self-defence, McDonnell Douglas published a pamphlet in June 1980 explaining the virtues of the DC10 and knocking its critics. The pamphlet did not contain any of the material used here. It claimed that the post-accident inquiries 'proved that the DC10 meets the toughest standards of aerospace technology'.

The pamphlet continued:

The DC10 is a carefully developed, meticulously engineered aircraft . . . . Eighteen million engineering man-hours were invested by McDonnell Douglas in DC10 development. This total included twelve million hours spent on design, four million on laboratory tests, and two million on flight tests. Sub-contractors invested additional millions of hours.

In developing the DC10 McDonnell Douglas conducted 14,000 hours of wind tunnel tests. Flight tests totalled 1,550 hours – the equivalent of hundreds of flights across the US. Full-scale fatigue testing of the DC10 provided the equivalent of 84,000 flights – 40 years of airline service.

Since the DC10 first entered airline service, McDonnell Douglas has invested an additional total of more than twenty-seven million engineering man-hours in product improvement. More than 5000 additional hours of flight testing have been conducted . . . .

The pamphlet continues in the same vein at some length. No doubt it is true, though it is still possible for mountains to labour and give birth to mice.

14
The plane must fly

If it does nothing else, McDonnell Douglas's *cri de coeur* on behalf of the DC10 at least explains something of the enormous investment which goes into the creation of a new airliner and the colossal pressures behind getting it certified and delivered to the customer on schedule. It is impossible to escape the conclusion that, at the design stage, the FAA's 318 aerospace engineers are incapable of excercising sufficiently close supervision over the 816 delegated engineering representatives (DERs) employed by US manufacturers. Especially since the latter frequently have more technical expertise than those who are supposed to be watching over them. In practice, only one in twenty of the decisions made by a DER on behalf of the FAA is reviewed by the authority according to its own guidelines – and there is some doubt as to whether even this low level of supervision is achieved.

One of the murkier areas of delegation is that of risk analysis – the process by which a manufacturer decides what might go wrong with the aircraft and how it should be guarded against. If this analysis shows that the likelihood of a failure or combination of failures is one chance in a billion, he can dismiss it as 'extremely improbable' and do nothing about it. There are two good examples of happenings deemed 'extremely improbable': one was the separation of the DC10 cargo door, the other the combination of events which brought down flight 191 in Chicago. So much for extreme improbability. In neither case did the DER employed by McDonnell Douglas think it worthwhile to pass on to the FAA the calculations on which the decisions had been made or, indeed, to mention that the possible failures had been considered and dismissed.

Nor are there any signs that the lesson has been learned. The Brooks Committee, referring to the Chicago disaster, reported:

This episode indicated that far from not inserting itself far enough into the design process, the FAA was not even aware that a transport category aircraft was type certificated on the basis of a risk analysis until after a catastrophe brought it to light. Even after the reliance on an 'extreme improbability' estimate was revealed, the FAA did not or could not examine the manufacturer's substantiation for the estimate. And even after the FAA's own consultant contradicted the manufacturer's risk analysis conclusion, the agency fundamentally misconstrued the meaning and underlying assumptions of the two risk analyses, recertified the plane, and resisted making changes that could reduce the risk revealed by the accident.

By implicitly defending the decision by only one of the three manufacturers of wide-body aircraft not to consider and guard against a particular, critical combination of failures, the FAA has demonstrated no perception of the fundamental problem. The decision to treat a potential failure as extremely improbable on the basis of a risk analysis is a basic regulatory decision. In order to ensure compliance with the regulations, not only must the FAA be aware that risk analyses are being used but must also review the basic assumptions, logic and methodology of those analyses.

It so happened that at the time this blast of criticism was being written, in Spring 1980, the FAA was involved with the final certification stages of another McDonnell Douglas project, the DC9 Super 80.

The Super 80 is, and is likely to remain, a controversial

aeroplane. Based on the widely used and long-established twin-jet DC9, it has been given more powerful engines and an enormously stretched fuselage to accommodate 172 passengers over short and medium distances. It is claimed to be quieter and more economical than its competitors and is certainly proving popular with the airlines. No fewer than eighty-five had been ordered before the first one left the production line. Two of the biggest orders have come from Switzerland and Austria.

But the enthusiasm of the airlines for a potential revenue-maker is not shared by the pilots. The Airline Pilots Association has been engaged in a running battle with the FAA over the certification of the Super 80, trying, without success, to involve themselves in the process. Rightly or wrongly, ALPA believes that the Super 80 is less than safe; some pilots have already threatened strike action rather than fly it. Their President, J.J. O'Donnell, said in a letter to Langhorne Bond on 10 January, 1980, 'There have been too many instances where the public interest has been given less than full measure of concern when weighed against the manufacturers' and airlines' motivation to reduce cost. There is a level of risk they are willing to accept which professional pilots the world over are not.' Why should one particular aeroplane from the drawing-board of a respected manufacturer cause such concern?

Out of three prototypes built, only one was left in flying condition when the FAA finally granted the type certificate in autumn 1980. As with all new aircraft in the US, the flight test programme on the DC9 Super 80 was conducted by FAA pilots. In the first incident, of which few details are known, the aircraft got into a deep stall – a fault to which designs with a high tailplane are prone – and was only saved when the pilot released the anti-spin braking parachute in the tail. McDonnell Douglas subsequently fitted a stick-pusher, which automatically brings the nose of the aircraft down if it should stall, but ALPA claims that this is confirmation that the Super 80 has undesirable characteristics. Why not, they say, go back and look at the basic design of the aircraft when such a thing happens?

ALPA's suspicion is that the tailplane is too small. Its engineering and operations manager, John E. O'Brien, certainly believes this was a factor in the second Super 80 incident which happened on 2 May, 1980 at Edwards air force base. The aircraft was being made to demonstrate its short-landing capability for the certification programme when it landed much too hard. The pilot, according to O'Brien, had the control column hard back to reduce the rate of descent, but it had no effect. Though the only injury incurred was to an FAA inspector, who suffered a broken ankle, the entire tail section of the Super 80 broke off in this accident and the nose undercarriage was also damaged.

For its part, McDonnell Douglas blamed the incident on pilot error and said it was pleased with the way the aircraft had survived the impact. The company would repair it and in the meantime carry on the certification tests with the two remaining machines, which actually belonged to Swissair and Austrian Airlines.

Just over six weeks later, on 19 June, came the second crash. This time the Super 80 was demonstrating its ability to land after a total hydraulic failure, which meant that the flaps, slats, anti-skid system, rudder boost and nosewheel steering were all switched off. It was a test demanded by the FAA because, after all, hydraulic systems have been known to fail. As test pilot George Lyddane touched down at 177 knots on the runway at McDonnell Douglas's airfield in Yuma, Arizona, the aircraft began to veer to the left.

He tried putting on right rudder, but without hydraulic power nothing much happened. So Lyddane tried a gentle dab on the right brake and put the right-hand engine into reverse thrust. Without the anti-skid device, the tyres on the right main landing gear burst. When he applied the left-hand brakes, the tyres on that side burst as well. The Super 80, now looking somewhat less than super, went off the runway into soft sand, sheered off its undercarriage and turned through 180 degrees. To add insult to injury, one of the two cranes which tried to rescue it later collapsed and punctured the fuselage.

To the casual observer, McDonnell Douglas now appeared to have a problem on its hands. There was one remaining prototype, the aircraft had failed two important certification tests in dramatic fashion, and they had a delivery schedule to meet. What was to be done?

The FAA permitted the company to repeat the hydraulic failure test, but said that this time it could allow the anti-skid units to remain in operation. Under the amended rules the Super 80 passed and was given its certificate of airworthiness in time to be delivered to Swissair on schedule. National Transportation Safety Board inquiries into the three test incidents had not been completed at this stage.

One of the major pilot grievances against the Super 80 – along with what they regard as an inadequate undercarriage and suspect low-speed handling – stems from the fact that it is designed to be flown by a two-man crew. This is an inflammable issue in cockpits the world over. The airlines, anxious to save on costs, claim that two-pilot operation is just as safe as having a pilot, first officer and flight engineer. Indeed, they can produce statistics, much challenged by pilots' organizations, to show it is even safer. Inevitably there are suggestions that the pilots are only trying to protect their own interest by keeping three men in the cockpit – a charge which is hotly denied by ALPA. For their part, the pilots claim that the extra workload on a two-man crew can lead to safety hazards, especially on short sectors which involve frequent communication with controllers and closely spaced take-off and landing checks. There is also the argument that an extra pair of eyes in the cockpit is valuable for keeping out of trouble in today's crowded airspace.

Anyway, with the advent of the DC9 Super 80, ALPA decided to put the matter to the test. It asked the FAA to conduct tests on the Super 80's cockpit by setting up a simulator programme to duplicate actual airline conditions. Since this was in 1978, there would have been time to iron out any problems before the aircraft reached the production line, and ALPA said that if the tests were satisfactory its members would fly in the two-man cockpit without further argument.

One might have thought that the FAA, understaffed and under attack for laxity and incompetence, would have welcomed this offer of expert assistance in the certification process. At the end of the day they stood to get industrial peace in the cockpit and, perhaps, a safer aeroplane. To nobody's great surprise, however, the FAA rejected the pilots' suggestion. The agency had, it said, no power to require the manufacturer to cooperate in such a scheme. Frustrated, ALPA went direct to McDonnell Douglas, which said blandly that it had no simulators available for such a task. ALPA regard this reply with frank disbelief, but there is nothing they can do about it.

The correspondence between the FAA and ALPA about the DC9 Super 80, which went on into 1980 and culminated in a demonstration outside the White House to demand Langhorne Bond's dismissal, makes interesting reading. Aside from revealing that the agency takes between two and four months to reply to quite urgent letters, it shows a scarcely concealed resentment on the part of the FAA that pilots should seek to meddle in the affairs of those who know best.

As the Brooks Committee found, any attempt to introduce outside expertise into the certification process for new aircraft is vehemently resisted by both the manufacturers and the FAA. Both claim that such a move would cause unnecessary delays and jeopardize manufacturers' trade secrets. Well, perhaps it would, though the committee found that safeguards would be easy to arrange. The important issue is whether such a disruption of the cosy arrangement between manufacturers and the FAA would lead to greater safety. The committee had little doubt that it would and was 'disturbed that the FAA seems to have made up its mind without fully considering the issue'. And just to prove the point, the committee ran its own inquiry on one vital piece of equipment which the agency had certified without bothering to ask the advice of the pilots.

The device concerned was the fail-passive autoland system (FPAS) which is fitted to Boeing 727 aircraft in order to enable them to land in poor visibility. It is a similar, but less expensive and sophisticated, system to that used in British Airways Trident aircraft; it is important to airlines who can improve profits and schedule reliability by landing in such conditions. The trouble with the FPAS is that if one component should fail (and they do) the system disconnects and leaves the pilot to make a manual landing.

This did not matter too much in the 1960s when the device was first introduced, because its use was limited to Category II conditions, that is, when runway visibility is at least 1200 feet and a decision on whether to land or go round again has to be made at a height of 100 feet – known as the 'decision height'. However, in 1976 the FAA decided to authorize use of the equipment in Category IIIa conditions – visibility of only 700 feet and a decision height of 50 feet. This was great news for the manufacturers, who were seeking to open up a market in newer aircraft such as the Boeing 737, but less good for pilots, who might now be expected to make split-second decisions very close to the ground.

The certification was made on the basis of the experience of the French (although they were using a different system incorporating a 'head up' instrument display) and on flight tests conducted in 1974 by Boeing and FAA pilots. These flight tests were not a full scientific investigation, and it was assumed by both Boeing and the FAA that 'all go-rounds will be successful, regardless of the height at which they are initiated'.

Was such an assumption justified? One pilot who gave evidence to the committee, Captain J.L. DeCelles, described the problems in the cockpit when trying to land in Category IIIa conditions. For a start, he said, the 700-foot visibility limit was measured as the distance at which a 2000 candlepower light would be visible – not quite the same thing as being able to see the ground. The pilot, travelling at around 250 feet per second, would probably see nothing until he was 70 feet from the runway. Then, in the two seconds taken to reach the decision height of 50 feet, he would have to decide whether to let the autoland system land the aircraft or to go round again. 'If we decide instantly at 50 feet – and if we do everything exactly right – then we probably won't touch the ground.' Pilots are unfortunately human, and the 'probably' was ominous, but there was worse to come.

Captain DeCelles went on, 'If, on the other hand we decide to continue the approach and at any time after 50 feet this system disconnects – and that is the thing that is unique about the fail-passive automatic landing system, that is, that it is liable to disconnect and, in fact, very liable to disconnect, and particularly at the point where the flare should initiate . . . you get a horn which says "You got it, buddy." You have a decision to make. You may be at 30 feet when the horn comes on, and then you have to decide very quickly if you are going to go around or if you are going to continue the landing manually.

'A decision like that, strangely enough, takes two or three seconds. At the end of those two or three seconds you are virtually on the ground.

'The FAA and the manufacturers say that this is no problem, because the worst that can happen is a hard landing. However, I happened to be behind an airplane that made such a hard landing at Los Angeles one night, and it burned up in the fog. Fortunately, all the passengers got out.

'So I cannot buy the idea that the worst that can happen is a hard landing.'

Captain DeCelles spoke like a man who knew what he was talking about. He was flatly contradicted by Mr Richard W. Taylor, vice president and special assistant to the president of the Boeing Company, who said his company had demonstrated that a flight crew could execute a safe go-round from any point in the approach. 'There is no problem with it whatsoever,' he said.

The committee was a touch sceptical. How had this been demonstrated?

By flight tests, said Mr Taylor.

How many tests? Mr Taylor said he did not know and offered to suply the information later. It took a lot of questions before Boeing finally came up with figures; these disclosed that there had been 350 flight tests – but made no mention of any of them having been made in Category IIIa conditions.

Like a dog with a juicy bone, the committee, to its

credit, would not let it go at that. In February 1980 they managed to contact two Boeing test pilots.

'Contrary to the statements and impressions given by Mr Taylor during the subcommittee's hearing,' says the report coldly, 'no such test programme had been conducted, on the grounds that it was unnecessary. This was confirmed during a previous staff conference with the then Deputy Director of FAA's Flight Standards Service.'

As the committee report points out:

This case illustrates not only why groups such as the Air Line Pilots Association wish to open up the certification process, but the potential dangers to the public of excluding them. A critical decision about the ability of flight crews to operate an important aircraft system was made without direct participation by those flight crews. Had ALPA been included in the assessment, it is likely that the FAA would have been forced to conduct the needed scientific programme of simulations. Such an assessment could have been made even more credible had the FAA selected at random average line pilots and tested their abilities to use the actual system in simulated conditions. The integrity of the FAA's decision-making in this instance could only have been improved by an open certification process.

It is clear that the overall situation in the United States, with a weak FAA susceptible to commercial pressures from the manufacturers and airlines, is highly unsatisfactory from a safety point of view. Committees sit, scandals are exposed, but nothing really changes.

But what of the rest of the world? With the exception of the Eastern Bloc and the highly successful European Airbus – which has an unblemished safety record at the time of writing – there are no large airliners now being produced outside the United States. However, each country has its own aviation authority; these have the power to demand changes in the American aircraft which are so often used by their airlines and, in some cases, they also have the technical ability to make their views stick. One such is the British Civil Aviation Authority. Required airworthiness standards in Britain are generally higher than in the United States and many American airliners require modification before they can be granted a British certificate. The Boeing 737, for instance, was known to be slightly unstable at speeds near the stall. The FAA found this acceptable; the CAA did not and insisted that changes be made to correct the tendency. They cost £100,000 per aircraft.

Three cheers for the CAA? Well, two cheers anyway. In the absence of congressional committees or a Freedom of Information Act, it is difficult to be sure that all is as it should be. Unlike the United States, where access to officials can be had by knocking on a door and questions are freely answered, appointments with the CAA have to be arranged in advance and interviews can only be conducted under the watchful eye of the authority's information officer. Documents highly relevant to air safety, such as Mandatory Occurrence Reports or the work of the Air Miss Working Group, are either completely unobtainable or doled out in a few carefully selected pages containing little of interest. Such inspissate secrecy undoubtedly disarms criticism; the danger is that it may lead to alarming complacency inside the authority itself.

Certainly there are some fields in which the CAA does not seem to be as energetic as it might be. In the constant battle between airline safety officers and their accountants, for instance, the authority ought to be wholeheartedly on the side of safety. Is it? John Boulding of British Airways says:

Sometimes the CAA will not back us. They don't seem to realize that if they will only indicate that they are going to make a procedure mandatory they will get it done a lot quicker.

The Chief Engineer has to justify expenditure. If he can say this is a mandatory modification it will be done without question. If he tells the accountant that it isn't, it may not be. If the engineer says "we may have an accident", the accountant will ask how many accidents have happened so far. The answer is "none". They don't realize that as time goes on we are running out of chances.

This is what we are running up against all the time. The CAA is an independent body. They could quite easily say that you have got to do something about this. We are going to make it mandatory, but we will give you a chance to get your aircraft modified first.

If they would only step in and proceed in that type of issue it would help the airlines no end. And the whole industry would get the advantage of it. It is no good, for example, British Airways taking action after problems with the BAC111 if the information doesn't get through to the other operators. We do try to tell them. Sometimes they take action and sometimes they don't.

A problem with the BAC111? Surely not; not with those stringent CAA airworthiness requirements. But there is. If this particular airliner has to make a landing without its flaps, perhaps because of a failure in the hydraulic system, there is a very fair chance that it will land on its belly. It happened at Stansted on 27 February 1978 to a BAC111 of Monarch Airlines, and it happened again on 26 September that year to a LACSA BAC111 at Miami, Florida. Fortunately no one was hurt in either accident, though the aircraft were severely damaged. Both were on training flights.

The reason for this potentially dangerous quirk is that the undercarriage warning horn, which alerts the pilot to the fact that his wheels are not down, operates through an airspeed scale. In a landing without flaps – which has to be carried out at the higher airspeed – the horn does not work.

The willingness of the CAA to control events in British skies was also called into question by a curious event which happened at Bristol's Lulsgate airport on 11 October 1979. The aircraft concerned was a Boeing 707 owned by a Swiss company, leased by an Indian business-man and carrying false Zaire registration numbers. It was flown from Helsinki to Lasham in Hampshire, where Dan-Air carried out some maintenance work on it – although the work the engineers were required to do still left sixty-two defects unrepaired. After twenty-six days at Lasham, the 707 left for Lulsgate, although the compasses were functioning poorly and neither high-frequency radio worked.

Of the three-man crew, only the flight engineer was properly qualified. The captain, Richard Rashid Khan Jr, had a revoked US commercial pilot's licence; the British co-pilot had only a private pilot's licence. Nevertheless, Khan had a good deal of talent with official paperwork, which extended to falsifying the aircraft's registration and insurance cover. No one seems to have inquired too closely.

From Lulsgate the 707 was due to fly to Kuwait *en route* to Bombay and it was duly loaded with 152,000 pounds of fuel. The flight engineer calculated that this would give them a take-off run of 7600 feet and Khan assured him that the runway was 7800 feet long. This was little enough margin even if true; in fact the Lulsgate runway is 6600 feet long.

Somehow the 707 managed to stagger into the air. As it did so it struck almost all the approach lights to the runway and carried away some hedges and a few pieces of tree into the bargain. The horrified controller, ever polite, radioed, 'Sir, do you realize what you have done?'

'No,' replied the pilot.

'You have damaged the runway lights, sir. There seem to be some pieces of aircraft as well. We will report back.' And so they did, after finding pieces of the flaps and several other odds and ends. But Khan flew on, to arrive in Kuwait with a three-foot metal bar protruding from a wing, branches in the undercarrriage and an air-conditioning bay full of metal debris.

The escapades of this rogue airliner continued round the Middle and Far East for months. It was last heard of in Ankara. But so far as its visit to Britain is concerned it seems pertinent to ask how an unfit aircraft with a false registration number and unqualified crew managed to escape any sort of official attention. The thing was a public danger. It could have crashed and caused great loss of life – and very nearly did. Yet if it had not struck those runway lights no one would have been any the wiser. The story says something about the cowboy operators who infest the lower end of the aviation industry. It says even more about the diligence and competence of the CAA.

15
The perils of fatigue

Before the late Neville Shute published his prophetic novel *No Highway* more than thirty years ago, few people had heard of metal fatigue. Shute was accused of scaremongering, but the accusers fell silent when the early Comet airliners began dropping out of the sky in 1953. Three crashes later, when metal fatigue had been firmly established as the cause of the Comet disasters, the British aviation industry and, it should not be forgotten, ninety-nine passengers and crew, had paid the price of pioneering. The British lead in jet transport was surrendered to the Americans, who had wisely profited from the mistakes and misfortunes of the Comet designers. It has never been recovered.

Slowly, as the years passed by without major accidents from this cause, metal fatigue became part of the past: a bogey consigned to the limbo cupboard of forgotten fear.

Nothing could be further from the truth.

Aeroplanes are still built of metal, and metal still becomes fatigued, corroded, cracked. What is more, the problem is growing, for whereas airlines in the 1950s would only keep their aircraft for six or seven years, the highly expensive jets of the present era may still be carrying passengers after a quarter of a century. Not, of course, with their original owners. By that time they will have passed through a number of hands, probably – though not necessarily, as we shall see – to the cowboy airlines and the poorer countries of the third world. The dangers of aircraft that are not only geriatric but also receive less than first-rate maintenance care impose no strain on the imagination.

Among American air carriers today, half the reported defects in airliners are structural problems. In the first three months of 1980, one major airline had eight serious fatigue or corrosion faults on five different types of aircraft. The one major factor which has prevented these worrisome cracks and holes from proliferating into a worldwide shower of aluminium and mangled bodies has been the development of fail-safe design. This means that in the event of the failure of a primary load-bearing structure, there will be another piece of metal available to take the strain. This is fine and dandy, but generally the secondary structure is not as strong as the first – and once the latter has failed there is no further back-up. Therefore unless the original fault is traced by inspection and repaired fairly quickly, disaster looms.

As it did on 14 May 1977 for a Boeing 707-321 cargo aircraft of Dan-Air at Lusaka, Zambia.

The Dan-Air flight, with a crew of five and one cargo handler on board, was carrying a load of freight from London to Lusaka via Nairobi. It was making the final approach to runway 10 at its destination, with flaps down and landing checks completed, when watchers on the ground saw the right-hand tailplane fall off. The outcome was inevitable. The aircraft dived vertically to the ground from a height of 800 feet, killing all six occupants instantly.

This particular 707 had been built in 1963 and had flown 47,621 hours, with 16,723 landings. It had been operated by Pan American as a passenger aircraft until March 1976, when it was pensioned off and put into storage in Florida. Three months later it was flown to the UK, where it was modified and overhauled by the Dan-Air workshops and given its British certificate of airworthiness on 14 October.

There was nothing in its history to telegraph its tragic end. While owned by Pan American it had been maintained to the approved FAA standards; since then it had been under the wing of the CAA. The aircraft had not been involved in any accidents, nor was there any record of an incident which might have damaged the structure. Nevertheless, the tail fell off.

Examination of the wreckage showed that the damage had begun with a fatigue crack at the top of the tailplane's rear spar. It had been there for a long time undetected, growing insidiously at the rate of one millimetre every 125 flights until the process speeded up and it failed completely. The remaining spars held the load for a while until they too fatigued under the stress of the bending tailplane and the whole structure gave way.

That there was nothing unusual in such a fatigue failure going undetected was quickly shown by the worldwide investigation of Boeing 707s which followed the Lusaka disaster. Of the 521 aircraft of this type operating in June 1977, no fewer than thirty-eight were found to have cracks of various sizes in the rear spars of their tailplanes. Four were so serious that the complete spar had to be replaced.

Clearly, something had gone wrong. To find out what it was, the diligent investigators of the UK Accidents Investigation Branch probed deeply into the design, manufacture and maintenance of the Boeing 707-300 series. What they discovered is a cause for some unease.

It transpired that the original Boeing 707, the series 100, had had fatigue tests carried out by the manufacturer before certification. As a result fatigue cracks were found in the tailplane rear spar, but only after 240,000 simulated flights. It was also proved that the rest of the structure was strong enough to stand the load.

However, when the series 300 version was developed, the tailplane was redesigned. Among other changes, the span was increased and the top surface covered with stainless steel instead of light alloy. The latter change improved the static strength of the tailplane; what was not realized at the time was that it would reduce the fatigue strength significantly. It was the first in the chain of events which led to the Lusaka crash.

No fatigue tests were carried out on the new tailplane. They were not considered necessary by Boeing, nor were they required by FAA regulations, which merely called for calculations to show that the strength was adequate. As for UK regulations, although they stipulated that 'parts which may be critical from fatigue aspects shall be subjected to such analysis and load tests as to demonstrate either a safe fatigue life or that such parts of the primary structure exhibit the characteristics of a fail-safe structure,' no such tests were asked for in the case of the 707-300. The Air Registration Board (later to become the CAA) decided to take the FAA's word for it.

The British authorities had, however, made one special condition before they granted the airworthiness certificate. Whereas Boeing had only recommended that this part of the aircraft be inspected every 21,000 hours, the ARB wanted the tailplane spar looked at after every 1800 hours of flight. However, even this was not sufficient to prevent the Lusaka accident; the rest of the structure could not sustain the load long enough to enable the cracked spar to be spotted in time.

One key conclusion drawn from the report on this disaster is that when aircraft designs are 'stretched' there must come a point when manufacturer and airworthiness authority decide that a complete review is necessary, instead of merely taking data from the existing model.

The report continues:

Persuasive arguments are regularly put forward by aircraft manufacturers and the airlines, that a modern aircraft designed to fail-safe principles should not be arbitrarily limited to a given service life, because feedback of service experience together with inspection would isolate problems before they become critical. The circumstances of this accident have reduced the weights of these arguments for two reason: the emergence of a long-term problem which had been totally unforeseen, and, secondly, the fact that it had remained undetected until brought to light during the investigation of the accident.

How many more 'totally unforeseen' problems are waiting to crop up? And how many manufacturers are taking the wise advice about the need for a complete review when aircraft are stretched?

All too often, the discovery of fatigue damage only comes after the event. On 17 September 1979, an Air Canada DC9 was over the Atlantic on a flight from Boston to Nova Scotia when it suddenly decompressed. The exit door and tail cone had fallen off because of a fatigue failure in the door jamb of the rear pressure bulkhead emergency exit. Luckily only one of the forty-three passengers and crew suffered minor injury and the pilot was able to return to Boston for an emergency landing. It could have been much worse.

Air Canada, which operates a large fleet of DC9s, immediately looked at the rest. No fewer than five were found to have fatigue cracks in the same area as the plane which came to grief and these were grounded until they could be repaired. At the same time the FAA ordered inspections to be carried out on all DC9s in the United States.

It is both curious and disturbing that such checks should have been necessary, because this was not an unknown problem. Back in May 1976 a service bulletin had been issued by McDonnell Douglas recommending that airlines should either strengthen the rear emergency-exit door on the DC9, or else conduct X-ray inspection every

4000 pressurization cycles. Air Canada had opted for the latter course and, according to McDonnell Douglas, the last X-ray taken of the plane which suffered the failure – 1000 cycles before the door fell into the Atlantic – showed cracks to be present at that time. Yet apparently nothing was done. Sometimes it does seem that the odds are stacked against the poor passenger. To fly in an aircraft which may suffer an unforeseen fatigue failure is unfortunate, but possibly unavoidable. To be in one which has a problem known to the manufacturer and detected by the airline but which is still uncorrected, is surely something he should not have to worry about.

Be that as it may, prior knowledge and even recent major disasters do not necessarily improve the eyesight of maintenance inspectors. Take the case of the engine which fell off a Pan American Boeing 747 as it landed at Heathrow airport on 27 December 1979. Only seven months after the Chicago DC10 disaster, it might be reasonable to suppose that airlines operating aircraft with engines hanging on pylons would be keeping a careful watch for faults. Yet the Heathrow incident happened. As luck would have it, no one was hurt on this occasion, though extensive fire broke out after the fatigue failure in the pylon bulkhead left the engine dangling within 10 inches of the ground. It was only discovered later that a similar fault had been found and corrected on a British Airways Boeing 747 some time before – and that the manufacturer knew about it.

The British Airways experience began in October 1976 when an inspector found a 1½-inch crack in the same type of bulkhead which later failed on the Pan American aircraft. The crack was stop-drilled and watched regularly from that point on, until in January 1978 it was seen to have spread to 4½ inches on one side of the bulkhead and 6 inches on the other. This was altogether too much. The

CAA was notified, the part replaced and the offending pieces sent back to Boeing. The manufacturer diagnosed the cause as 'overload' – possibly a heavy landing or a collision with a truck – though nothing in the aircraft's record suggested anything of the sort had happened. Boeing did not bother to pass the news on to other operators and no airworthiness directive was issued by the CAA.

After the Pan American incident at Heathrow, however, both Boeing and the FAA acted as though fire-crackers had been set off beneath them. The latter actually telegraphed an airworthiness directive on the very next day, demanding a visual inspection for cracks if loose fasteners were discovered. Twelve pylons on 747s were in fact found to have loose or missing fasteners – which presumably would have been spotted earlier if Boeing had not decided to sit on the information.

The fact that such faults so frequently remain undetected until someone has an accident must call into question the efficiency of airline maintenance. This was another area looked at by the Brooks Committee report of April 1980, with predictably disturbing results.

The committee found serious deficiencies in the performance of essential maintenance by some US airlines, often arising from the need to keep the aircraft flying and earning money. They heard abundant evidence from mechanics of the pressures exerted on them to take short cuts. Said one, 'Everyone is one is on your back to make flight schedule. Often pressure is exerted to do a sixty minute job in fifteen. Even the foreman always wants you or tells you to take short cuts and don't do portions of the checks. This is common practice in the airlines today. There is threat of closing maintenance at the station if too many delays occur. The saying is – "Just get the flight out, you can always find some way to sign off a write up." Also, I have seen foreman say, " If it is not in the log book they can't prove anything." '

In a poll conducted among its members by the mechanics' union, the Aircraft Mechanics Fraternal Association, in June 1979, there was a clear indication that the men had no faith in the ability or willingness of the FAA or their quality-control departments to halt this intimidation. In all, sixty-one per cent said the FAA gave them the impression of being part of management; eighty-six per cent said they felt the FAA would take the word of management above theirs and only twenty-three per cent trusted the FAA. Asked whether they felt they would be protected if they informed the FAA about safety or airworthiness violations, seventy-five per cent said 'No'. One man added, 'I was threatened after I reported a violation. Many times I have called the FAA, but there has been no action. The Company and the FAA live in incest.'

In such circumstances, it is easy to see why faults go unnoticed until too late and why prompt warning is not given to other carriers that their aircraft may be at hazard.

Such blatant gambling with the lives of passengers ought, in theory, to be impossible. Each airline has to have by law a quality-control department, which itself is subject to checks by the FAA in the United States and the CAA in Britain.

In Britain the system may work – that is to say I have no hard evidence to the contrary. In America it certainly does not: seventy-nine per cent of mechanics claim that their quality-control department is 'always being intimidated by management not to write up discrepancies', and the FAA inspectors are much too thin on the ground to do much about it. In the southwest region, for example, there are six inspectors to oversee an airline that employs 6000

mechanics and they also have to look after the investigation of near-miss incidents and inspect hazardous
materials. In Britain, the CAA has 81 inspectors for 8,550
maintenance engineers – a ratio of 1 to 106. In 1975, the
ratio was 1 to 54; the level of CAA supervision has halved
in six years.

FAA spot checks, known as systems worthiness
analysis programme (SWAP) inspections, are something
of a joke. Airlines are always given advance notice of the
inspectors' arrival and the committee had documentary
evidence that at least one company, American Airlines,
advised its maintenance supervisors to purge their files in
order to hide problems from the SWAP team. The same
company gave its employees a twenty-page brief on the
standard replies to be given to FAA inspectors. These
were designed to keep as much information as possible
secret.

'This is clear evidence,' says the committee report, 'that
these audits are not plausible enforcement tools. It also
raises serious questions as to what the posture of the
airlines is during the months or years when no FAA audit
is pending.' Indeed it does.

However, the FAA is not always deceived. One SWAP
report on Eastern Airlines in 1974 accused the management of 'at times practising false economy when it comes
to maintaining their aircraft. The central theme seems to
be : postpone corrective action on defects as long as possible. . . . It seems to be the rule rather than the exception,
that items pertaining to airworthiness are carried over,
often until the next phases check or beyond. . . . It appears
to be standard practice to defer many inspectors' findings
during phase inspections until the next scheduled inspection (approximately 1500 hours and five to six months
elapsed time).'

A 1977 report on American Airlines found that not only

had inspections been delegated to mechanics but that quality-check inspectors had not even received formal training on the aircraft they were supposed to be checking. 'The lack of formal training for mechanics can be very dangerous,' said the Brooks Committee. 'Inadequate training clearly contributed to the faulty maintenance of the pylon assembly of the Chicago accident aircraft. It is intolerable that those who are to inspect the results of "on the job" training, also have no formal training.'

The FAA can also have teeth. Following an investigation of its maintenance procedures which began in 1979, Braniff Airlines was fined $1,500,000 – which gives a fair indication of the seriousness of its violations. Among other things, the FAA found that Braniff was stalling in giving information to its inspectors and taking 'adverse action' against mechanics who refused to sign for work which they knew was unacceptable. The investigation demonstrated, said the committee in a withering comment, that 'even a scheduled carrier can have a "compliance disposition" worthy of a non-scheduled "cockroach corner" operator.'

Yet the situation is getting worse, not better. Since 1978 the SWAP inspection teams have been reduced by one-third and not even the Chicago accident has persuaded the FAA that in future it ought to be notified of changes in maintenance procedures. The action which the FAA can take against an offending airline or manufacturer ranges from revocation or suspension of a licence to a fine, a letter of correction or a warning notice. The trend is toward the less severe penalties. In 1979, letters or warning notices accounted for sixty-eight per cent of the FAA's actions, compared with fifty-four-and-a-half per cent the year before. It is hard to believe that the threat of finding one of these in the mail strikes much fear in the heart of the errant companies.

16
May all your problems be little ones

Be it a fatigue crack or a misheard instruction, a moment's inattention or a faulty instrument, most air disasters have small beginnings. And if the passengers are lucky, the sequence of events may go no further. An accident has been defined by one humourist in the industry as ten things going wrong at once, an incident as nine things going wrong at once, and air safety as only eight things going wrong at once. Hardly the sort of thing to put on the airline brochures, but not too far from the truth.

The strangest things can happen. Witness the case of the Tristar 200 which operated for three weeks in the spring of 1979 with stiff ailerons. Each time the aircraft landed, the crew complained about this difficulty – which made the plane hard to control – but inspections of the cockpit and the below-deck flight control linkages revealed nothing wrong. In spite of the pilots' complaints, the Tristar continued to fly hundreds of unsuspecting people around the United States. Finally, on 17 May at Atlanta, Georgia, the maintenance department was persuaded to have a more thorough look. They found a splintered piece of 2- inch by 4-inch wooden board 4½ feet long, jammed into the right wing close to the inboard aileron-control cable bellcranks. The last maintenance work in that area had involved the replacement of a support fitting for the undercarriage. The wooden board, suspected the maintenance supervisors, might have been used as an unauthorized tool. The situation was roughly analogous to a surgeon leaving his scalpel behind after the operation – except that the death toll in this instance would have been rather higher.

Another Tristar was flying between Miami and New York on the evening of 11 January 1980 when a six-year-old boy was seen to be making frequent trips to the lavatory. The stewardesses took no notice – small boys can be that way – until after his final visit the lad charged down the gangway yelling 'Fire.' Luckily there happened to be a fireman among the passengers. Responding to the call of duty, he ran to the toilet and found heavy smoke, with a fire burning in the door of the tissue compartment. He searched in vain for a fire extinguisher, then gave up and put the fire out with water. Afterwards, a good many spent matches were found on the floor. The reaction of the boy's parents is not recorded but they, and everyone else on board, could count themselves lucky to survive.

Passengers can certainly cause their share of trouble, ranging from the bizarre to the downright disastrous. In the former category was the young lady on a trans-Atlantic jumbo who found her own solution to the problem of clothing fire-hazard by stripping naked after slight over-indulgence in the first-class champagne, and parading starkers through the tourist section. In-flight entertainment has rarely been so popular.

At the other end of the scale was the passenger on board a BAC111 of Phillipine Airlines *en route* to Manila on 18 August 1978. Having taken out a heavy insurance before the flight, this gentleman locked himself in the toilet and exploded a bomb. He was sucked out through the resulting hole in the fuselage and fell into the Pacific 24,000 feet below. It says much for the British Aerospace product that the pilot was able to make a successful emergency landing – and much for the laws of chance that the same thing had happened to the same aircraft three years before.

The same sort of explosive decompression might well have happened to a British Airways Tristar on the Dhahran to London run on 8 December 1979, only this time it would have been the flight crew who made an abrupt exit. While on the ground at the Middle East airport, the crew had opened the escape hatch in the roof above their heads in order to get some fresh air. There is a warning light in the Tristar cockpit to warn the pilot if this hatch is not properly closed, but this had been out of action for several flights because there were no spares available. The hatch was shut before take-off and checked by the flight engineer; what he did not know was that a torsion spring was broken, which prevented it locking correctly. As the Tristar sped down the runway, the hatch came open and the take-off was abandoned. If the failure had been delayed until 35,000 feet, the story might have had a different ending.

It was not the first time such a thing had happened to British Airways. On 6 September 1978, Flight BA20 – a Boeing 747 routed from Calcutta to Muscat, was well advanced on its take-off run when an increasingly loud noise was heard on the flight deck. The take-off was abandoned at 125 knots and the aircraft returned to the apron, where it stayed because several tyres had over-heated and deflated. The noise was traced to the fact that the flight-deck hatch was not securely fastened; it had presumably been opened to cool the crew while the 747 had been delayed at Calcutta with air-conditioning problems.

Two months earlier, on 5 July, severe decompression had in fact happened on board a British Airways 747 over the Atlantic when the pressurization system failed. Flight 271 from London to Boston was two hours from its destination at 35,000 feet when the pressure in the cabin fell to the equivalent of 29,000 feet. The 252 passengers and eighteen crew suddenly found themselves breathing air thinner than was necessary to retain consciousness. One woman's heart stopped but she was revived with mouth-to-mouth resuscitation and heart massage. It was a good moment to find out whether the emergency oxygen masks for the crew were attached to their cylinders: they were not. Most, but not all, of the oxygen masks for the passengers came down from their ceiling panels; but some passengers panicked because the bags on the masks were not inflating fully in the way shown in the pretty pictures on the safety leaflets. Actually the pictures were wrong, and have since been changed. It was some minutes before anyone on the ground knew that this incident had happened: the pilot, co-pilot and engineer all became temporarily deaf and could not communicate with each other or the controllers.

Slightly less serious, but distinctly unfunny at the time, was the case of the Pan American captain's shirt collar. The incident happened while his Boeing 747 was cruising quietly over Brazil on 26 November 1979 *en route* from Rio de Janiero to Miami. All systems were operating normally, the speed was Mach 0.84 and the jungle was 35,000 feet below. The captain decided to visit the lavatory. He was tieless and with his shirt collar open as he returned to the cockpit to get back in the left-hand seat. As he did so, he felt a pull on his shirt and the number one engine stopped. His collar had caught in the emergency fire handle, extinguishing the engine with great efficiency. Fortunately they were able to relight the engine two minutes later.

The needs of commerce, as we have seen already, are sometimes at odds with those of safety. Even so, no airline would knowingly dispatch an overloaded aeroplane, and the pilot of British Airways flight 278 from Miami to London on 24 August 1978 was puzzled to find that his DC10 seemed to be tail-heavy. He got the aircraft to

London safely but there was a surprise waiting for him when he arrived. As well as the 481 kilograms of baggage which the load sheet showed to be installed in the rear number four hold, there were an additional four trunks and seven wooden boxes, plus 200 kilograms of mail. In all this weighed 1430 kilograms. With around a ton too much in the tail, no wonder the captain had had problems.

The cause of the trouble was a gentle piece of arm-twisting carried out on British Airways by an American construction company which was about to commence a contract in Jeddah. The construction team would be a large one, a valuable account, with both first-class and tourist passengers winging their way between Miami and Jeddah for a long time to come. An advance party of eight engineers was booked on flight 278; to ensure the company's continued patronage, perhaps British Airways would take a generous view of their excess baggage? The airline acquiesced without a murmur and no excess charges were made. Indeed, it seems doubtful that the stuff was ever weighed, since the engineers craftily brought it along in small lots and no one seemed to realize that construction tools are heavy.

One can get away with a lot when times are hard, but British Airways are resolved to be a little more careful when making this kind of concession in future. They may have been uncomfortably aware that only three months before at Miami, on 25 May 1978, a Convair 880 of Groth Air Services had failed to take off because it was incorrectly loaded. The Convair overran the runway and was completely destroyed.

Aircrew are only human – which should be fairly obvious by now – and like the rest of us they get tired from time to time. The flight engineer of a British Airways Super VC10 *en route* from Hong Kong to Tokyo late in 1974 was very tired indeed. It was logical when the aircraft began to show signs of imbalance that he should switch the fuel feed system so that all four engines were drawing from number four tank on the heavy side of the plane. It was unfortunate that he was so tired that he forgot to switch them back again.

They were flying at 37,000 feet, high in the night sky above the South China Sea; with only twelve passengers on board the VC10 had a sort of eerie, cathedral-like emptiness, which became more pronounced when all the engines stopped. With them, of course, went the generators which powered the lights and, more important, the major flying controls. The aircraft began to glide downwards at 3000 feet per minute, rolling from side to side with bank angles as high as 45 degrees. The pilot tried to send out a mayday call, but without power it is doubtful if anyone heard him. He was confined to emergency lighting and stand-by instrumentation as he turned through 90 degrees of the airway and struggled to discover what had gone wrong.

There was one device left to help him – and luckily it worked. The VC10 has an emergency ram air turbine which, when lowered from the fuselage into the slipstream, can generate enough power to get most of the flying controls working again. This was done, the fuel feed switches were moved from the now-empty number four tank, and the engines restarted at 28,000 feet. By which time it seems a fair bet that everyone on the flight deck was fairly wide awake.

Like all the other stories in this book, that one comes from documented sources. It has to be admitted that the following one does not, but as it originates from Mr Homer Mouden, vice-president of the Flight Safety Foundation in Washington, DC, there is no reason to doubt its veracity.

Mr Mouden is a spruce sixty-eight-year-old former airline pilot who served with Braniff Airlines for thirty-two years and then joined the flight safety department of Eastern Airlines for five years before taking up his present post in 1977. It was while he was with Eastern that he was woken up one night by a very shaken pilot. It was small wonder that the pilot was upset: he had just had the fright of his life.

The incident had happened northwest of Palm Beach, Florida, at a point where the airways intersect at a radio navigation beacon. This fact ensures that there is always a healthy flow of airliners through the spot travelling in different directions. The radio beacon itself sits on a small airfield, and the airfield is used by sky-divers.

Unknown to the pilot, who was flying a DC9 with a load of passengers on board, it was being used by sky-divers that night. As he came to the intersection at 6000 feet and began to make his inbound turn to Palm Beach, something flashed by very close to the cockpit. A parachutist free-falling from 13,000 feet had missed the aircraft by perhaps 30 yards. With the DC9 travelling at several hundred miles an hour, another fraction of a second would have seen him hit the wing – which would undoubtedly have killed himself and everyone else.

Incredibly, the sky-diver was within his legal rights. Under a regulation passed by the FAA when it was under the control of a Mr Hallaby – who was interested in parachuting – sky-divers in the United States can operate when and where they like, provided they notify the FAA. They then get a permit which is good for twelve months. It is all part of the freedom of the skies, though why anyone should wish to parachute through a crowded airway beggars the imagination. Mr Hallaby is long gone but the regulation still survives. So, by chance, do the passengers and crew of the Eastern Airlines DC9.

The FAA reaction to this incident was interesting. It asked Mr Mouden to supply it with the number of the aircraft and the name of the pilot so that it could 'file a violation against him'.

'That's the attitude that bothers me,' Mr Mouden said. 'I feel that they should first of all have a training programme and alert system so that these people won't go out and kill themselves and a lot of innocent passengers. If a human body hit the wing of an aeroplane it would take it off.'

To end this chapter on a lighter note, one cannot but admire the sang-froid of the average airline passenger. The poor fellow has to put up with a lot, though few have their calm tested in the same way as those on board a British Airtour Boeing 707 on 14 December 1978. Flight BA559 had just touched down at Heathrow and the big jets were roaring in reverse, when a meal trolley at the back of the aircraft broke loose from its moorings. Like a driverless bobsleigh, the bulky cart charged down the full length of the centre aisle, aiming itself with deadly precision at the cockpit door. Door, trolley, and a full load of dirty plates finished up on top of the astonished crew, who none the less managed to complete the landing safely. The passengers released their seatbelts and climbed out. As they left the aircraft, thanking the shaken stewardesses who stood beside the awful carnage, not one of them made the slightest comment. Perhaps they thought it was all part of British Airways' entertainment service.

17
Survival kit

The edge of the cliff for aviation safety is not far away. The reasons are many, but exacerbating all of them is the economic distress being suffered by the airlines as part of the world recession. In 1980 the major operators lost more than £1000 million, as falling traffic, rising fuel prices, and savage competition that forced them to cut fares, bit deeply into their revenue. Passengers who revel in the cheaper travel now available may find their delight short-lived. Though it is true that the dead protectionist hand of IATA had kept fares at an unrealistically high level for too long–and still does on many routes–there are signs that the pendulum may have swung back too far.

Air safety does not come cheap, and we have already seen how reluctant some airlines can be to obey the rules when it costs them money. If they act in such a manner when the industry is relatively prosperous, how will they react when every pound and every dollar spent sends them further into the red? The answer could be, perhaps should be, that they will have no choice – that firm regulation and supervision by government agencies will ensure that they toe the line. Anyone who believes that is living in cloud-cuckoo-land. Governments are short of money too; both the CAA and the FAA have suffered cutbacks in their inspection staff in recent years. Without sufficient inspectors on the ground – and inspectors of sufficient calibre – the temptation for airlines to skimp on essential maintenance and their opportunities to do so will be great.

Ironically, one of the greatest dangers aises from the very fact that the modern jet airliner has become so much more reliable than its piston-engined predecessor and that the number of crashes (though not their severity) has fallen as a result. This has bred a slumbrous air of complacency in the industry, from which it is only awakened by such incidents as Chicago or Tenerife.

One man who is highly concerned about the future is Charles (Chuck) Miller, who learned about safety the hard way as a testpilot in the U S for fifteen years and later became director of the NTSB's Bureau of Aviation Safety. Since becoming a peripheral casualty of the Watergate scandal in 1974, Miller has been running his own safety consultancy from his home in McClean, Virginia. Though he already held a Bachelor's degree in aeronautical engineering and a Master's degree in systems management, he recently went back to school to get a law degree – at an age when most men would be thinking of retirement – in order to fight the system more effectively.

Not many people know, or care, more about air safety than Chuck Miller. 'I'm scared,' he says, 'because I know the kind of stuff that's going on at the NTSB. I've seen what's going on at the FAA, and I know there is a two-, three- or four-year lag before we see this showing up in operations. I think we're going to be in a hell of a mess in two or three years. It wouldn't surprise me a bit to see a flock of major accidents in 1981.'

Miller's prime concern, echoed by many others in a postion to know, is the lack of expertise among those who control aviation in the United States. 'What happens,' he asks, 'when the people who are calling the shots in a reasonably technical area like aviation don't know their arse from first base?' He quotes an example. 'In 1979,

anyone who talks about the visual inspection of parts in a
high-performance aircraft, as Langhorne Bond did after
the Chicago crash, is out of his cotton-picking mind.'

Miller is highly critcial of the NTSB for what he describes as their 'once over lightly' approach to accident
investigation and for their refusal to allow outside experts
(like himself) to participate in investigations if they represent claimants or insurance companies. Though there is
undoubtedly an element of special pleading in this, Miller
is supported to a degree by Homer Mouden of the Flight
Safety Foundation, who strongly dislikes the NTSB's
emphasis on finding the 'probable cause' of an accident. In
Mouden's view it is not the 'probable cause' – which could
be, for instance, the aircraft striking the ground – which
matters. He believes that what should be investigated are
the contributory factors which led up to the accident,
especially the human factors.

It may well be that, as with the argument for opening up
the certification process for new aircraft, the addition of
outside expertise to accident investigations would lead to
safer flying. Yet the introduction of lawyers into the air-
safety imbroglio is highly controversial. Supporters of the
idea, like Miller, argue that lawyers are needed to stand up
for the rights of the individual passenger and that if they
are denied access to factual information such people get
hurt. 'It irritates me,' he says, 'to hear people say that
lawyers get in the way of safety. I can tell you some cases
where if the lawyers hadn't got in the way you would have
had some rather severe injustices. To put it another way:
there is a vacuum being developed by this poor investigation work by our NTSB that the lawyers are going to fill.'

Maybe so, but it is easy to see why the idea of legal
intervention strikes terror in the hearts of airlines and
manufacturers. The Turkish Airlines DC10 crash outside
Paris led to payment of $60 million dollars in compensa-

tion, and claims against McDonnell Douglas and American Airlines for the Chicago disaster already total more than $1000 million – though the final settlement is likely to be much less. Fair enough, say the legal protagonists: the fear of being hit so hard in the wallet will make these people doubly careful in future.

The argument is strong, but it misses the basic point that no one deliberately crashes an aeroplane. It tends to be bad for business. Accidents are often caused by an accumulation of small things – none of them fatal in themselves and many of which have been experienced by other operators at other times.

What is desperately needed is a worldwide network of information so that pilots, mechanics and everyone else in the industry can see exactly what is happening. Lawyers stifle this process, because everyone is frightened to reveal their own mishaps or shortcomings for fear that the information will be used against them in court. This fear is far from imaginary: it has happened. Manufacturers have even been inhibited from making safety modifications to aircraft because there would be an assumption that the part to be replaced, although representing the state of the art at the time it was designed, was being admitted to be unsafe.

Attempts have been made in the past to set up such a clearing-house of information. The Flight Safety Foundation, to which 110 airlines throughout the world subscribe, once ran a system under which it received incident reports from its subscribers, de-identified them, and passed them around. But eventually it fell foul of the lawyers and the supply of information dried up. The ASRS system in the United States and the UK's Air Miss Working Group are both attempts to achieve the same thing on a limited scale. But the de-identification process used by the former is so extreme that it robs its reports of almost all meaning, while the secrecy practised by the latter means that many people vitally involved in the industry are left in ignorance.

It is not so much the information about accidents which matter, though this is important, but a wider knowledge of incidents, of system errors in air-traffic control and detected structural faults. We need to know about the things which only just failed to go wrong and then think ahead to accident prevention if we are to break the endless chain of complacency followed by disaster, followed by panic and recrimination.

Ideally, all this information should be fed to a central computer, from which it could be distributed to operators and manufacturers the world over. It should also be made available to the public by being open to press inquiry. Though such a suggestion will be anathema to both authorities and industry, there could be no better method of keeping all concerned on their toes than the knowledge that those who buy the tickets know what is going on. The idea is Utopian, of course. It will never happen. There are no great technical problems, but political and commercial objections can be relied upon to see that any such scheme is still-born.

Fear is the key: fear of the consequences of being found out. Until some system can be devised whereby all those at the sharp end – the pilots, controllers, engineers and mechanics – can confess their sins without fear of retribution, human nature will prevail. Such a scheme has in fact operated in Australia for the past forty years, and with great success, but the adoption of any such system by the major flying nations seems as far away as ever. There seems to be a greater concern with discipline than with stopping the next accident.

Freedom of information, in the widest possible sense, would be the biggest single contribution towards reducing the steady toll of air disaster. Short of that, there are other things to do.

There is a need, for example, to pay much closer attention to the 'why' of accidents, rather than merely investigating how they happened. Very few do not involve failure of the human factor at some point in the sequence to disaster, yet little is done in this field except by the Royal Canadian Air Force, whose intensive methods might well repay study. There is nothing safer than an airliner when it is sitting empty on the tarmac; it is only when a man climbs on board that the thing becomes dangerous.

Allied to this is the need to stop overloading the vulnerable man in the cockpit. In theory, increased automation has made his task much easier; in practice it does not always work out like that. The more gadgets there are on the flight deck, the more things there are to go wrong. Furthermore, the increasing use of two-man crews with the elimination of the flight engineer will put an added strain on the pilot when the electronics go on the blink.

There is also a tendency, for commercial reasons, to use each new advance to increase the utilization of the aircraft, for example the use of autoland systems in bad visibility. From a safety point of view, this pushes the passengers back to square one. Longer runways have been suggested as a safety precaution, but experience has shown that when these are provided the operators simply put more payload in the aeroplanes.

Not that the provision of new airports and longer runways – both important for safety – is an easy matter. Planning inquiries and the protests of environmentalists can hold up such progress for years, as the delay in providing a new airport for London has shown all too clearly. The objections are understandable, but for those who fly they mean packing more and more aircraft into the same overcrowded airspace. One day the crunch will come.

The problem of controlling the growing amount of air traffic is a crucial one. In Britain the standard is generally high, as it is in the United States, though mistakes are made in both. Elsewhere the picture is very mixed, with the greatest area for concern in the countries around the Mediterranean where so many British holidaymakers fly. Lack of ground-control radar facilities is almost universal and, in some countries, the controllers are under-paid and under-trained. Add to that the widespread refusal to stick to the rules and use English as the lingua franca of the air, and the extra responsibility thrown upon pilots becomes plain.

The situation is made vastly more complicated by the fact that each country in Europe guards its own airspace with the jealous zeal of a medieval baron in his castle. Though an attempt was made to break the log-jam with Eurocontrol, based in Maastricht, this has become little more than a bureaucratic irrelevance. The apparent logic of having a single authority to control the safe passage of aircraft over the whole of Europe has so far evaded the panjandrums in Brussels.

There are things which can be done to improve air safety, but before they can begin there is an urgent need to sweep away the cobwebs of complacency and recognize, before the problem gets worse, that it does exist. The purpose of this book has not been to frighten but to inform – to lift a corner of the curtain so that those who fly for business or pleasure can learn a little more of what goes on.

Flying will never be totally safe. The air is an alien element to man and should be treated, like the sea, with wary respect. That is every reason for making the unsafe sky as secure as we can make it. Which means a great deal safer than it is today.